Deep Governance Matters

The world of community service and mission

BY KATHLEEN DONNELLON

Published in Australia by
Garratt Publishing
32 Glenvale Crescent
Mulgrave, VIC 3170
www.garrattpublishing.com.au

Cover Design by Guy Holt
Text Design by Garratt Publishing
Illustrations © iStock
Edited by Greg Hill
Cover image iStock

ISBN 9781922484468

Cataloguing in Publication information for this title is available from the National Library of Australia.
www.nla.gov.au

The authors and publisher gratefully acknowledge the permission granted to reproduce the copyright material in this book. Every effort has been made to trace copyright holders and to obtain their permission for the use of copyright material.

For Tom and Lola

Deep Governance Matters is a wonderful resource for the rapidly growing number of directors and council members involved in oversight and governance of not-for-profit organisations, especially those that are faith-based. It clearly and accessibly sets out important principles, illustrating them with many concrete examples. New board members will be encouraged by many helpful suggestions and tips, while more experienced directors will look at some of their own experiences in a new light. Deep governance does indeed matter, not only because of what can go wrong, but because it directly impacts how well an organisation pursues its mission. This book will help promote high quality governance and greater effectiveness by not-for-profit organisations throughout our community.

– Bishop Shane Mackinlay

Kathleen Donnellon has created a terrific resource. This is a really clear and engaging book on such an important topic. The anecdotes are excellent: candid and insightful.

– Virginia Bourke
Pro Chancellor, Australian Catholic University, Chair of the Board of Mercy Health

The first thing that is clear when reading this book is that Kathleen has been there, at the grassroots of NFP Governance, and fully understands, at depth, not only all that is to know about the intricacies of faith-based governance, but also the psyche of those about to embark on such a serious responsibility. I wish I'd had the advantage of this tool to navigate such a labyrinth of information, nuance, peculiar language and personal emotional probing before I stepped into the world of mission-based governance.

I applaud the distinction between corporate and faith-based NFP and cannot agree more about the emphasis given to mission and relationship. These are the defining features of our sector. Kathleen has ensured that they permeate every aspect of governance.

This book has clarity of material, is encouraging, enlightening and engaging, and follows a logical sequence in structure. It is serious in nature and light in approach. It leaves no stone unturned, thus opening up what has often been an area where we could only come to understand our commitment and responsibilities when already well on the journey. Kathleen has made a contribution of great importance to prospective board members and those of us who have been seasoned over many years.

– Mary Louise Petro, RSM
Congregational Leader, Sisters of Mercy, Parramatta

Deep Governance Matters casts a contemporary light on faith-based ministries with a tone which is pithy, honest and engaging. While at first glance it appears deceptively simple, at no stage does the reader doubt that this book is written by someone who has a deep experience of Boards – and in particular Boards that govern a faith-based mission. *Deep Governance Matters* encompasses a lot of common sense, for example, *Who runs the organisation – the CEO or the Board?* Many such apparently simple questions are asked, and the answers provided in this book show that they are often not the simple questions they first appear to be.

– Brigid Arthur csb, AO
Founder and Project Coordinator, Brigidine Asylum Seeker Project

Deep Governance Matters is perfect for anyone thinking of joining a mission-based Board. Too often people are scared to join a Board for the first time or think, 'What do I have to offer and will I fit in?' This book helps demonstrate that Boards need people of diverse backgrounds and experience and there likely is a role for you.

This is a great read, as it reinforces and reminds us (even a current director in a mission-based organisation) of the importance of our mission in the work that we do. Kathleen's personal stories really help to bring to life the nuances of a mission-based Board and the important role that governance and the Board plays in working towards that mission.

– Travis Bowman
Chair Finance Risk and Audit Committee and Director, Mercy Works

This book covers everything you've ever wanted to know about governance and mission. *Deep Governance Matters* is an engaging and heart-warming read on what could be a heavy topic. It is written with a light touch, great insight, and practical guidance.

Kathleen lives out all this accumulated wisdom – I can vouch for that! I had the privilege of working as an Executive Director alongside Kathleen as my Board Chair. She has an agile mind and a great capacity for building relationships which is evidenced in the style of this book. I felt very moved when I realised I may even be counted as one of Kathleen's 'radical women' friends in the chapter *Do I have to behave like a 'nun'?*

– Sally Bradley RSM
Executive Director, Mercy Works

Deep Governance Matters is entertaining, accessible and practical – full of stories, examples and advice for life on a not-for-profit Board.

This is a book you can dip into again and again – before you join a Board, when you're faced with tough decisions, and when you need some inspiration and motivation. With short chapters on topics such as risk management, the importance of diversity, and strategic planning, Kathleen draws on her extensive and diverse real-life experiences to share how to 'keep mission as your compass'.

If you're about to join a board, or if you're feeling jaded and wondering what it's all about, this book is for you. Inspiring and entertaining, filled with real life stories and practical advice, Kathleen helps us to feel better about our ability to contribute to good governance, and teaches us how to stay sane along the way.

– Lisa Dwyer, Chair Star of the Sea College Board,
Deals Strategy and Infrastructure Advisory, PwC

God of all time
We are grateful for
the dreaming
the courage
the openness
that has brought us to this place
this time of now.

May we, with energy and hope,
embrace the possibilities you offer us.
May we be ready to
listen and learn,
question and challenge,
imagine and envision anew.

May our hearts hear your insistent call
and be enlivened by its promise
of one world, one sacred community,
one body in the cosmic Christ.

Amen

Anne Young

Contents

Foreword by Michael McGirr 1

An Acknowledgement of *Acknowledgement of Country* 5

Introduction: There's a big difference between sitting on a board and sitting around bored 9

1. What, exactly, is a board? 13

2. What sort of people become board directors? 19

3. What is governance anyway? 23

4. Why does governance matter? 27

5. Do I have to behave like a 'nun'? 31

6. Why all the fuss about 'mission'? 35

7. Is mission more important than governance? 39

8. What questions should I ask before starting? 43

9. Will everyone be older/younger/smarter than me? 47

10. Are there risks involved in joining a board? 51

11. Why is the terminology so confusing? 57

12. What if I can't stand another board member? 63

13. What do subcommittees do? 67

14. Am I the only one feeling confused? 71

15. Should I join if the organisation is a bit run down? 75

16. How much time will it take? 79

17. Do I need to be a parent to be on a school board? 83

18. How do I find out what's going on? 87

19. Do I have to agree with everyone else? 91

20. What is a fiduciary duty? 95

21. What is 'formation'? 99

22. Is strategic planning really boring? 103

23. Will I get paid? 107

24. What if I feel overwhelmed? 111

25. Who runs the place – the board or the Executive Director? 115

26. The board chair – how hard can it be to run a meeting? 119

27. Will I have to 'lean in'? 123

28. What on earth is an MPJP? 127

29. What happens if the members (or owners) disagree with the board's decision? 131

30. We've done 'mission', so can we start work now? 135

31. Did someone mention a pilgrimage? 141

32. Why does board history matter? 145

33. Did someone say synodality? 149

34. What's in it for me? 153

Reflections and prayers 157

Glossary 163

Epigraph Bibliography 170

Suggested Links 174

Bibliography 175

Acknowledgements 177

Foreword

I have many weaknesses. One is a penchant for corny old jokes. Here is an example …

A distinguished art critic wanders into the first exhibition of a young painter. The crowds recognise him and part to let the personage come through. He sniffs at a few paintings and then finds the budding artist, drawing himself up to his full height.

'Do you want my opinion of your work?' he asks her in a patronising manner.

'Okay,' says the artist.

'It is absolutely worthless,' he replies.

'Fine,' replies the artist. 'But let's hear it anyway.'

What has this old gag got to do with governance? Well, when you think about it, the joke is about power. The critic assumes that all the power belongs to him and the people who act deferentially only consolidate a dysfunctional situation. The artist finds her voice to make a more level playing field. Good on her!

Governance is about sharing responsibility, about listening to a range of opinions rather than just those of the so-called important people. When structures of governance work well, nobody is passive or disengaged or disempowered. There is no division between critics and artists. Everyone is working together to create a single glorious work of art.

Deep Governance Matters, The world of community, service and mission is a wonderful book. It deals with precisely this kind of situation. It challenges groups that become dysfunctional because only one voice matters or because they don't have a structure that is strong enough to properly bear the weight of their responsibility. Governance is a big word. It makes people think of rules and regulations and long documents. It may also make people think of contesting visions in conflict with each other, even of power games.

Kathleen Donnellon knows it doesn't have to be like that. She is a lawyer with years of experience on boards and in consultancy, especially in the not-for-profit sector where mission, rather than money, is the key motivator. There are countless stories and insights in this book that remind us that governance involves human beings trying to achieve important purposes. Kathleen is enormously encouraging, practical and entertaining. She shows that governance is a task that lies within the capabilities of more of us than we may have imagined. Governance is closely related to mission. The mission is our why. Governance is our how. They need each other, just as a great idea needs a structure to bring it to reality.

Governance is far from arid. It can be creative and even fun. But for this to happen, it needs to take place in a secure and supported structure where roles and responsibilities are clear, transparent and accountable. Kathleen knows first-hand that more of us need to take an active part in the management of the schools, hospitals, day-care centres and social institutions on which our community relies. Done well, governance can be a most rewarding experience. In communities with religious origins, there is a slow but steady maturation away from 'the pastor knows best' to 'we all share our mission'. We all have to be, at different times, both artists and critics.

The broader context of this book is important. We live in a world that often feels fragile and tense. Humans are slow learners and in some parts of the world we have once again seen the rise of dictators who are hell bent, to use a phrase advisedly, on treating everyone else as pawns in their game. Closer to home, people no longer trust institutions that have served us well for centuries. There are people who are keen to tear down structures without having anything meaningful to put in their place.

This book helps to change this. On the one hand, it shows us ways us to move from individual power to group responsibility and creativity. On the other hand, it calls more of us to step up to take our part in strengthening structures that our community needs now and in the future.

The word 'governance' owes its origin to the sea. It comes from the Latin word for piloting or steering a ship, something that requires skill in both good weather and bad. This is worth remembering as Kathleen Donnellon invites us on a voyage of discovery where we need all hands on deck.

– ***Michael McGirr***

An Acknowledgement of
Acknowledgement
of Country

I grew up on a farm on Dja Dja Wurrung land in central Victoria. As a child, I often regretted that our local region was completely devoid of Aboriginal history. I don't mean that I didn't know the history, but that I believed there was none. I actually romanticised about what it would be like living on land that had been part of an ancient culture and I envied people living in remote northern Australia – where I imagined all the clans had lived. I had no understanding of the Indigenous history of the land on which I was raised or that the same land that gave me such deep solace and peace, had also given deep solace and peace to countless generations of First Nations people.

Or it did, until the arrival of the white settlers, who included my own Irish ancestors. They, along with their countrymen and women, had fled the famine that killed large numbers of dispossessed and marginalised people in Ireland in the mid to late 1800's. One despised people found their salvation in the subjugation of another.

My naïve fantasies – about needing to be in northern Australia to be able to stand on land that had been cared for by an ancient culture – were well and truly misplaced. It's now painful to know that the land that I loved and that nurtured me, was denied to the people who had nurtured it for so long. In 2013, a Recognition and Settlement Agreement was entered into between the Dja Dja Wurrung Clans Aboriginal Corporation (DDWCAC), and the State of Victoria, which recognises the Dja Dja Wurrung people as the traditional owners of that land and acknowledges that their people had a continuous relationship with it for over one thousand generations. It also acknowledges the suffering endured by Dja Dja Wurrung ancestors at the time of colonisation – including unrecorded murders and dispossession. It gives the Dja Dja Wurrung rights in respect of the land, including the right to practice culture and manage Country.

I have lived in my current city home (on Bunurong land) for twenty-four years now, and there have been other homes in between. But 'home' to me, still means that land that cared for me when I was young and vulnerable. My parents were the first generation of our family to live on our farm. The Dja Dja Wurrung had been its custodians for one thousand generations before us.

Welcome to Country ceremonies and *Acknowledgment of Country* statements have become largely mainstream in Australia. They occur at concerts, in schools, in parliament, at festivals, and at sporting events. An *Acknowledgement of Country* is now a part of each board meeting that I attend. On a personal level, I want to regularly acknowledge First Nations people as the original custodians of this country. Good governance is relational, and Welcome to Country ceremonies reflect for me the complex understanding that the traditional owners have had, for thousands of years, of the value of respectful relationships.

These rituals have some detractors though, including some First Nations people who see them as tokenism at best, and detracting from the real issues affecting Indigenous communities at worst. Certainly much more needs to be done in a practical way, to address the harm that has been wrought on First Nations people. They remain second-class citizens in their own land – overrepresented in prisons, underrepresented in all forms of leadership, and with health outcomes inferior to other Australians.

Our various sporting, social and work communities and organisations continue to include Welcome to Country or Acknowledgement of Country at the commencement of proceedings. They do this in good faith – in the understanding that they are supported by most traditional owners – and they trust that they do so in a way that is meaningful, inclusive and respectful. I've learned my lesson, however, in overestimating my own understanding of First Nations culture. These are not my traditions. I'm the coloniser. I need to continue to heed the voice of First Nations people themselves. I need to keep listening.

Introduction:
There's a big difference between sitting on a board and sitting around bored

We all need schools, hospitals, aged care facilities, community support organisations and all sorts of other social institutions. But they don't run themselves!

This book is written to help people who may have been approached to become directors of a not-for-profit board or council, people who are thinking about sharing such important work, and people who might just be wondering what that meeting on a Wednesday night is all about.

In my parents' time, it was common to volunteer with organisations like Vinnies or the Lions Club, where the work was hands-on and often very community-based. These and similar organisations still do great work – and all power to the people who give up their time to help their communities in this very practical and useful way.

But times have also changed, and we now look to ordinary people to not just do the hands-on work but to guide some of that work. We've come to think of many of these 'caring' organisations as just being part of the furniture – always there to reach out to our community members in need. But these schools, hospitals, refugee-support bodies, community care centres and suchlike, can only continue their tradition of care with the support of people like you: people prepared to take on the responsibility of ensuring good governance, so that all who rely on them will be able to continue to do so. The role of governance is more important than ever. It is not always easy to find people who have the time, expertise, and confidence to fill these leadership roles. Often, people are inclined to underestimate what they have to offer. The word 'board' can make people think of the Reserve Bank or some listed company where directors are handsomely paid. Good luck to them. But this book is about a different world, the world of community, service, and mission. You may be paid for your efforts, but you probably won't be. Great opportunities and experiences will come your way regardless.

I would like to offer this book as an encouragement and even inspiration. I have spent many years as a board director and also as a board chair of not-for-profit, church-based ministries. These have included the board of a large catholic school, the board of a Christian-based, international development organisation, and the board of an order of Catholic sisters.

I love this work. It supports the structures that in turn support our young people, our frail, our people living with disabilities, our refugees, our First Nations people, our traumatised, and our most marginalised. To become involved in this work is to walk respectfully alongside all marginalised people. As for what skills you need to do the work, I trained as a lawyer and mediator, but to be honest, what I learned as a mother, community member and person of faith is as important to the work as my professional skills.

The stories in this book are mostly about organisations grounded in the Christian tradition with a particular focus on Catholic ministries. That's been my area of experience. There are, of course, many other faith traditions that also undertake this great work. At heart, we share a common mission of outreach and support for people in need.

This is not a book that details the rules for governance and the responsibilities of a board. It is important you understand these things and I will suggest a few links that might help you to that end.

Rather, for those who have recently been asked to join a board, or who have recently done so, I see this as offering a bit of light while you are standing in the tunnel and wondering what you might find at the other end. For those who are experienced board directors, perhaps this will offer new perspectives. I have some stories to share. I will also share with you some of the questions that I wish I had asked when I first became involved in this work. I hope to answer some of the FAQs that are often thought, but seldom actually asked.

1

What, exactly,
is a board?

In the beginning…

Genesis 1:1, NRSV Bible

In the first year that I taught Dispute Resolution at the University of Melbourne Law School, a student came to me after a class spent discussing a decision of the Federal Court and murmured self-consciously that she didn't know what the Federal Court was. It was a salutatory lesson for a new lecturer. My students were all graduates of previous degrees, and I had made a presumption that they (as first year law students) would have acquired a basic working knowledge of the structure of the legal system along the way. Lots of them had – but lots of them hadn't. From then on, although it wasn't part of the curriculum, a rundown on the hierarchy of courts became a standard inclusion in my lectures.

I suspect the same uncertainty might apply to becoming a board member in a faith-based, not-for-profit organisation. So, this section is for anyone who wants to murmur self-consciously that they don't really understand what a board is, or what it does.

What is a board?

A board is a group of people who have been appointed as board directors by the members of a company. The board is responsible for the proper functioning of that corporate entity. It is an important role and carries significant responsibility. It shouldn't be taken on lightly. There are risks involved in being a company director, including being company director of a faith-based not-for-profit.[1]

The directors who make up the board define the specific purpose or mission of the organisation (in the foundational documents) and create the strategic plan for achieving that purpose. The owners of the company

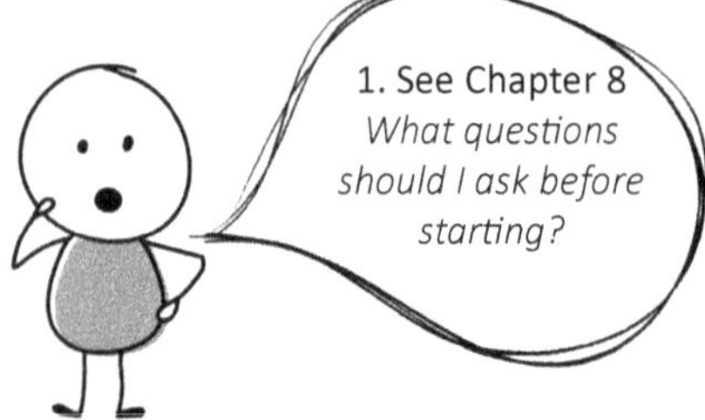

(in our case likely to be a religious congregation or a diocese or a MPJP, but we'll come to that later) will have defined the broad mission goals in the company constitution. While it's the company directors who create the foundational documents[2], they do so in alignment with the mission of the owners.

The board then oversees execution of the strategic plan by the operational arm of the organisation, namely the management team and staff, who are led by the Executive Director (or CEO). The Executive Director (or CEO) reports to the board at each board meeting.

What happens in board meetings?

The decisions that have the most significant impact on your ministry, are made in board meetings.

Meetings will always involve discussion of the reports made to the board by the subcommittee(s) and the Executive Director. The reports will have been made available to the board directors at least a week before the meeting, to give them the opportunity to read and fully consider them. This is part of the oversight and monitoring role of the board. The meeting then provides the opportunity for directors to ask questions or seek further information or clarification on those reports.

In not-for-profits, the board should also have a mechanism for ensuring that all decisions made by the board are consistent with the mission of the ministry. There are different ways this can be achieved, but all involve ensuring that all board members are 'on board' with mission.[3] For that reason, part of the board agenda might sometimes be given to

providing *formation* for the board.[4] This can be as simple as a short prayer or reflection (in Australia, this would come after an *Acknowledgement of Country* or *Welcome to Country* when appropriate), and on occasion, might involve a day or half-day set aside for more in-depth reflection.

One of the major discussion points will be about strategic planning, which is the responsibility of the board. How do you go about doing what you're there to do? You might sometimes devote full days to strategic planning, as it's such an integral part of what the board does, and will be an integral part of many of the discussions at the board table. Does a new opportunity that has just arisen fit within mission and strategic outlook or not? A pivotal staff member has just resigned. Do you simply replace that staff member, or use it as an opportunity to reconsider your staffing needs, in light of your most recent strategic plan?

Often boards will have guests present at meetings. These might be staff giving a short run-down on their role in the ministry or perhaps partners who either work with the ministry or who benefit from the work done by it. On a school board I was on, we had both students and staff members give regular reports to the board. These contributions give board members an insight into the operation of the ministry that they can otherwise feel quite detached from, as board members are not involved in the day-to-day operation.

Are all boards the same?

Different risks and responsibilities apply to different types of governance structures. Following is a very quick rundown of the primary structures used by not-for-profits.

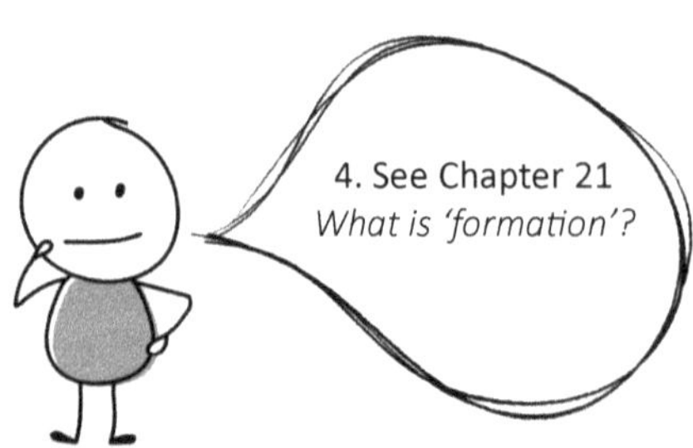

Advisory Boards

As the name suggests, an advisory board is a group of people who provide advice to the owner of an organisation. They do not have power to make decisions for the organisation, and this means that they are not legally responsible for the decisions that are made by the owner. Parish primary schools, for example, often have advisory boards.

Incorporated Associations

Incorporated associations are often created for state-based, not-for-profit organisations. They are a legal entity and can own property and enter contracts. They are required to have rules of association, which set out the purpose of the organisation and define how it will operate. Any profit made must be used for the purposes of the association. They are created under state rather than federal law, and so they are best suited to organisations whose purpose does not cross state borders. Board members have limited liability.[5]

Unincorporated Associations

An unincorporated association is not a legal entity in its own right. These associations are made up of a small group of like-minded people who create a committee for the purpose of working towards a common goal. Sporting clubs are often unincorporated associations. As they are not separate legal entities, there are no legal requirements for rules or procedures, although the group may decide to write some. For example, if an unincorporated association wants to rent a property, the lease must be taken out in the name of an individual member (or members). This creates a risk of personal legal liability for the lease holder(s).

Company limited by guarantee

Faith based not-for-profits often operate through the structure of a company limited by guarantee. Companies limited by guarantee are established in accordance with the requirements of the Australian Securities and Investment Commission (ASIC). Charities are also required to register with the Australian Charities and Not-for-profits Commission (ACNC). Regulatory requirements are more strict for companies limited by guarantee than those that apply to incorporated associations, although companies registered with the ACNC have slightly less rigid requirements than for-profit companies.

The company is created by 'members', who are the owners of the company.[6] Board members have limited liability.

Proprietary Company limited by shares or Public Company limited by shares

These are not structures used by not-for-profit organisations.

They are 'for-profit' entities, where ownership of the organisation is by shareholding.

What sort of people become board directors?

Great actions speak great minds, and such should govern…
Beaumont and Fletcher, *The prophetess*

Sometimes people are reluctant to put their hands up to become board directors, because they're a bit fearful that they'll end up looking silly. They get concerned that they won't have anything worthwhile to offer the board. It's certainly true that boards need good directors with strong skills. However, boards need people with a wide range of skills, and the skills that are needed, are not always the ones you immediately think of.

Background first. Directors are (usually) appointed by the members or owners of the company, and not by the board. It's likely however, that the board will have made a recommendation to the members that new directors are needed.

Board directors are responsible for overseeing the running of the company, for example in the areas of:

- mission
- strategic direction
- risk management
- overseeing financial accounts
- ensuring regulatory compliance
- defining, monitoring and evaluating culture.

The composition of the board will vary, depending on the nature and size of the ministry. To comply with civil and constitutional obligations, boards require expertise in a range of areas. Depending on the nature of the company, this expertise might include:

- mission
- finance/accounting
- legal

- risk management
- climate change risk management
- ESG (environmental, social and governance) practices
- strategic development
- change management
- public relations
- human resources
- information technology
- governance
- compliance
- safeguarding
- professional expertise relating to the business of the company
- personal experience, as someone who has benefitted from the work of the company
- many, many other possibilities.

Probably more important than any one of those specific skills, however, is the need to have a range of directors who are:

- relational
- strategic
- negotiators
- clear thinkers
- lateral thinkers
- creative
- courageous
- collaborative
- have good judgment

- insightful
- robust
- keen to be at the table
- available to contribute the amount of time that is required of board and/or subcommittee membership.

Don't discount what you have to offer as a director simply because you might not have industry experience in the area of work that the board operates in. A disability support organisation might need to have people with disability support work experience on it, but it certainly doesn't need only those skillsets. Boards need a broad range of skills, perspectives, experience and wisdom.

3

What is governance anyway?

... all things should be done decently and in order.

1 Corinthians 14:4, NRSV Bible

Governance is shorthand for the processes we have in place to ensure that an organisation runs safely, efficiently, and effectively. A well-governed entity has structures that enable transparency, accountability, and integrity in operations and in decision-making. In not-for-profit ministries, it encompasses mission, strategic planning, policies and procedures, reporting lines, risk management and more. It's important for organisations to get their governance systems right. They are the safety valve that should prevent disaster due to poor decision-making. Think about an organisation you've read about in the media recently who have had half their board resign *en masse,* or who have been ordered to pay huge fines or who have their board Chair and their CEO disagree in public, and I'll show you an organisation that needs to work on their governance systems.

This book is not a detailed 'how to' on governance. Governance is a big topic, and there are lots of great resources available to assist boards and management teams in implementing and maintaining good governance systems. (The links and references at the end of this book will provide you with further information). For you, as a prospective or new board member, there are a few key points to remember when it comes to governance, especially in faith-based ministries:

1. Governance is not structure for structure's sake.

Governance is an essential function of the board. It's necessary for your board and management team to be on top of this fundamental aspect of board responsibility. However, governance is not the reason your ministry exists. Your ministry exists because of your mission. Having good governance processes, however, helps your organisation to achieve the best possible mission outcomes.

There is a difference between good governance and 'governance for governance sake'. Occasionally, organisational leaders can become so mired in structures that it can feel as though the ministry exists to support the governance system, rather than that the governance system existing to support your mission. Implementing structures for the sake of having structures (unnecessary and inefficient meetings; 'tick the box' feedback/review; unnecessary committees) is poor governance. It's the tail wagging the dog. Good governance is implementing structures and processes that support the effectiveness, efficiency, transparency, integrity and accountability of the organisation, which is what ultimately results in the best possible mission outcome.

2. Good governance is relational

The ability to engage well with people is by far your strongest governance asset. Having strong risk management and formation structures won't protect you, if you can't communicate well with your colleagues, partners, and other stakeholders. Above all, good governance is relational.

3. In a faith-based not-for-profit company, governance must encompass mission.

The obvious difference between publicly listed companies and not-for-profit companies is that one is there to make profit for its shareholders, and the other is there to support the community in some way. The heart of a not-for-profit ministry is its mission, which is its reason for existing. There must be structures in place to ensure that mission is embedded throughout the organisation, in the same way that there must be structures to ensure financial oversight, compliance, safeguarding and the like. Updating your company mission statement doesn't entitle you to declare 'mission done!' for the next twelve months. Mission is ongoing.

Governance structures supporting mission can include:

- regular formation
- mission-based decision-making criteria
- mission-based strategic planning
- board and/or subcommittee members with mission expertise.

A significant aspect of governance is the requirement for incorporated boards to report to their members (owners). It's likely that your board Chair will be in regular contact with the members throughout the year in relation to numerous matters. This information flow has practical benefits for both the board and the members and is also a way of ensuring that the members and the board remain largely on the same page. Good governance is relational! Each year, there is also likely to be an Annual General Meeting (AGM), when a formal report is provided to the members. The report will, amongst other things, highlight key achievements, explain any budget anomalies, and set out plans for the future.

The report should also detail the ways in which the ministry's achievements that year, align with its mission. If it transpires that the outcomes are not aligned with the mission, then the board has a problem. Board members are stewards of mission and are accountable for that stewardship to the company members (and also to other stakeholders such as donors, partners and volunteers).

Mission is the reason that all of you are there.

4

Why does governance matter?

You shall not, for the sake of one individual,
change the meaning of principle and integrity.

Jane Austen, *Pride and prejudice*

If we want to look at why governance matters, we needn't look any further than at the Australian Royal Commission into Institutional Responses to Child Sexual Abuse.[1] The Commission shone light into the grimiest corners of the Catholic Church (and other institutions) in Australia and found utter devastation. Individuals who should have protected the most vulnerable members of their community, instead betrayed them by engaging directly in physical and/or sexual abuse. People who should have prevented the abuse either ignored it or protected the abusers for the sake of avoiding reputational damage to the church. Other individuals (priests in particular) who were *not* involved in any way with the abuse or the cover-up, were tarred with the 'abuser' brush that has since, inevitably, swept over the whole institution. Faithful, lifelong churchgoers have stopped going to mass, because they no longer wish to be part of an institution that betrayed its own so violently and corruptly and for such a long time.

The Church, through the new body, Australian Catholic Safeguarding Limited (ACSL), has responded to the criticisms made by the Commission by rolling out detailed safeguarding processes (processes designed to protect vulnerable people) to apply to all its ministries. Compliance (regulation of those processes) is an important part of the answer. History has shown, with clarity, that meaningful safeguarding measures are essential in creating environments where children and at risk adults are safe from predators. These measures include such things as policies providing clarity around behavioural expectations, establishing reporting procedures, and defining forms of abuse and the like.

But safeguarding is not the heart of the issue. The heart of the issue is how the mission of the church could collapse so spectacularly when it came to the need for protection of vulnerable children and adults.

1. Australian Royal Commission into Institutional Responses to Child Sexual Abuse: https://www.childabuseroyalcommission.gov.au/

The collapse of mission cannot be 'complianced' away in the form of safety checklists and policies. Compliance is a tool of governance, and governance is a process for the effective running of an organisation. Governance processes should have protected the vulnerable from predators and didn't. The far more stringent safeguarding processes that have now been put in place are a risk-management tool providing structures that we hope will prevent any such wholesale breach being repeated. But different governance processes should have underpinned mission. How, in any single case, much less over hundreds of cases (or thousands worldwide) was reputational damage prioritised over child safety? What happened to the gospel value of outreach to the marginalised?

This failure can be categorised as a failure of culture, particularly in the way that clericalism, or the notion of the exceptionalism of the ordained, was permitted to flourish. But what was it that brought about that culture of clericalism, that culture that led so many amongst the clergy and the clerical hierarchy to accept that protection of the clergy and the church was paramount? It was surely an egregious failure in living up to the mission of the gospels – a mission that should have left no room for a code of exceptionalism within its ranks.

Women and men in religious life, and we the laypeople alongside them as workers and leaders in church ministries, are all 'formed' or trained in the mission of our organisations. This is not just part of an induction package. Formation is an ongoing process intended to ensure that mission remains at the heart of all we do.[2] What happened to formation throughout the church? Where was the oversight? Where was Christ in any of the decisions that failed those vulnerable people? These are profound mission and culture failings, and mission was failed by the governance processes that should have supported it.

So, governance matters.

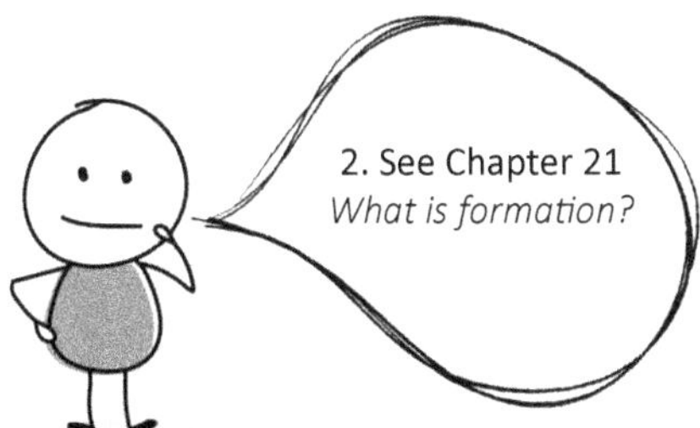

5

Do I have to behave like a 'nun'?

My idea of good company, Mr Elliot, is the company of clever, well-informed people, who have a great deal of conversation.

Jane Austen, *Persuasion*

Well, for starters, if you're asking this question, you probably need to readjust your image of what 'nuns' (or 'sisters') are, and how they behave! 'Nuns' are women who take religious vows and live a cloistered life of prayer. Women who have taken religious vows but live active lives within the community, are generally referred to as 'Sisters'.

Recently, I was asked to be on a panel of 'Radical Women', who had been gathered to speak to a group of Year 9 students at a Catholic secondary college.

It got me thinking about the concept of radicalism and I started wondering which of my friends were the most radical. It turns out that my most radical friends are Sisters. Who'd have thought? The concept of 'nuns' as radicals flies in the face of the conservative, traditional way in which they are frequently portrayed in the media. Yet my friends often experience deep, eye-rolling frustration, at being lumbered with that reactionary image.

My friends are women who spend their lives advocating for asylum seekers and refugees. They are entirely accepting of diversity (including gender and sexuality). They do not talk about God all the time and nor do they universally refer to God as 'he'. They willingly admit that they have more questions than answers about God. They do believe in God and that God is universal love. They live the values of the gospels. They work for ever and ever. I have served on boards with Sisters into their 80s, who continue to work diligently and effectively for the benefit of marginalised people. They speak out against misogyny. They speak out against injustice, and they walk alongside the people who suffer from it.

Most Sisters no longer wear habits or live in convents. They know that their way of life is dying out and they have the grace and courage to not just accept it, but to embrace that change. They work to enable others to take on leadership of the various forms of outreach that they have created and managed, and to which they continue to contribute.

My friends have loved the freedom that being a Sister has given them. The notion of 'freedom' in religious life feels a little counter-intuitive for most of us when that religious vocation demands poverty, celibacy, and obedience, but that's their experience. They have been leaders of huge organisations. They have travelled and worked internationally. They feel frustration at times with their community, and they love sharing the hope, love of God and support of each other that is unique to such a community. They continue to live lives of action, prayer, reflection, and community. My friends are radical women.

So, if after all of that you think you're up to the job of behaving like a 'nun', more power to you!

As to whether you need to take on the faith, duties and responsibilities of being a member of a religious congregation, then the answer is a clear 'no'. There are many directors of faith-based ministries who do not share the faith tradition that guides the ministry. You must, however, accept and support the mission of the ministry. This includes ensuring that the mission of the organisation is embedded in policy and in practice and is lived throughout the organisation every day.

6

Why all the fuss about 'mission'?

What do we live for, if it is not to make life less difficult for each other?

George Eliot (Mary Ann Evans), *Middlemarch*

Why are we here?

It sounds a bit existential, but when it comes to being on a board, a director should be able to give a pretty good answer to that question within a couple of sentences and the sentences provided by the different board members should be largely interchangeable. For faith-based ministries, it's not a simple matter of saying 'to educate' or 'to heal' or similar phrases, because that's only part of the story.

In a faith-based ministry, mission is the heart of what your organisation exists to do. It's your compass as you navigate your way through decision-making. Education or health or community service might be your business, but the way you go about doing that work is defined by your mission. By way of example, why do we still have faith-based schools? If it's only to educate – we could leave it to the state. Why *does* your ministry continue to exist as a faith based ministry? It's a question that you should have on the table, in some form, at every meeting.

Hopefully, your board has a well-considered answer! It's important that board directors are aligned on mission because if they aren't, they cannot be effective. What does 'success' mean if there are different perspectives on mission?

Technically, there are two separate-but-related 'missions' that you're signing up for.

1. The mission of the owner, or member of the company.

This is the historical, philosophical, theological, and spiritual context in which your organisation was established, and continues to exist.

For example, let's say you agree to become a director of a school established by the Loreto Sisters, and that school is now governed by Loreto Ministries Limited. Mary Ward founded the Loretos in the early 1600s. If you join the board of a Loreto school, you will engage in ongoing professional development about how and why the Loreto order came to exist, and about how and why it continues to exist. Part of the Loreto living mission is to empower students to advocate for positive change. This mission is imbued throughout all its ministries.

2. The company's mission, as set out in its Mission Statement.

Your ministry will have its own mission statement. While the statement will be grounded in the mission of the owner or member, it will be specific to the work of your company. For example, if you have joined the board of a faith-based health-care organisation whose owner's mission is outreach to the vulnerable, your company's mission statement might include that it will provide compassionate and accessible health care to the vulnerable in the community.

Your mission statement shouldn't be a 'set and forget' motherhood statement. The work you do in your ministry comes back to your mission statement and values. The terms 'compassionate' and 'vulnerable' in the above example are there for a reason. In a committee meeting, when you're robustly discussing whether to build a new building or to start providing assistance to a different group within the community, or when to close down a program that has been running for a long time, your decision will be grounded in your mission.

This statement (and the accompanying documents and processes, including your values and vision statements) must *walk the walk* as well as *talk the talk*. If your proposed mission statement would apply just as well to the organisation down the road, you need to head back to the drawing board, because the work just hasn't been done.

Saying that your ministry produces outcomes that are 'exceptional' or 'inspirational' doesn't make it so. What does 'exceptional' mean to your board in the context of your mission? Drill down. In a nursing home, for example, it might mean creative support of the individual patient. There are so many potential forms of 'exceptional' care provided in this context. Work out what they are and form them into your mission. Don't settle for platitudes. Platitudes will not impact upon the people reading your website, and they give no direction or inspiration to your board members in their decision making.

Your board should periodically revisit your foundational documents including your mission, vision and values statements and when necessary, renew them as part of your ongoing strategic process, to adapt them to contemporary circumstances. Your mission goal must, of course, remain within the umbrella of the mission of the company members. Ensuring alignment between the company mission and that of the company members is an ongoing task for the board. This task is made much more straightforward, of course, if the board (and particularly the board chair) has regular dialogue with the members.

Your mission is your reason for being.

Is mission more important than governance?

If you have built castles in the air, your work need not be lost; that is where they should be. Now put the foundations under them.

Henry David Thoreau, *Waldon*

I once had a heated exchange in a meeting – involving numerous board chairs and trustee directors of a Ministerial Public Juridic Person (MPJP)[1] – during which a frustrated trustee told me that 'governance doesn't matter'. That brought the conversation to a close. I didn't have the first idea of how to even begin to respond to her. There are layers of ways in which governance matters: accountability, transparency, and integrity for starters. Of course, the trustee in question knew full well that all those things matter. What she was really saying was that, where there's a contest between governance and mission, mission must win.

This can be an attractive argument, the 'when it comes down to it, process doesn't matter, outcomes matter' argument. But it's false logic. Clear reporting lines, nimble risk management processes, strong compliance structures, collaborative and relational decision-making and a mission focus in all board and committee deliberations, serve rather than hinder the purpose of the ministry. In fact, without such processes in place, mission is at risk.

I was Chair of the board of a not-for-profit ministry whose only form of income was donor funds. As a board, we voted to sack our largest donor. Let's call him Fred. We didn't have a queue of Freds lined up to take his place. We all knew that losing Fred would leave a gaping hole in our finances. We took months to make the decision. We took it only when it became crystal clear that Fred's vision for improving the lives of the people we worked with, had moved a long way from our vision. Fred's

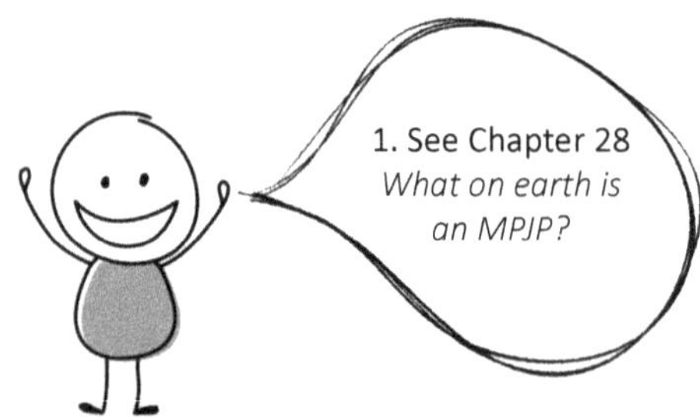

intentions were good, and we had done good work with project partners with his donations. But Fred's funds did not come unencumbered.

Fred had supported our organisation over several years because we had a long history of working with marginalised people, and we had project workers on the ground to implement and oversee our programs. We worked in collaboration with our project partners: the people we were supporting and assisting.

Fred had clear criteria about the projects that he was willing to fund. Over the years, those criteria changed and narrowed. We had our own criteria for determining what programs we would support; they had been developed collaboratively with our project partners. Over time, the projects that we were required to support with Fred's funds were not projects that fitted the criteria that we had created jointly with those partners.

We tried very hard to work with Fred to find alternative programs that would be acceptable to all three of us: our ministry, the partners we were working with, and Fred, but Fred was committed to his own path.

It took us a long time to come to our eventual decision. Part of the reason is that one of our responsibilities as directors is to ensure the financial security of our ministry. On the face of it, sacking our largest donor was madness. In the end, however, the decision became simple, because continuing to accept the funds for projects that didn't fit our criteria was in breach of our mission, and therefore contrary to our strategic goals. We voted to sack the donor.

I am glad to say that our ministry did *not* fold as a result of this difficult decision. In fact, staff found that once their desks were cleared from what had become known as 'Fred's work', space was cleared for 'our work'. Our donations manager had time to spend on the core of his work, and while I can't honestly say that new donations flooded in, they certainly flowed in.

Governance is not an end in itself: it is the tool we use to achieve effective outcomes. It was our governance processes (our program criteria) that ultimately enabled us to make the mission-based decision that supported rather than encumbered our strategic plan. Governance is not more important than mission. It's there to support mission (and to support the effective running of the organisation as a whole). But without good governance processes, mission is at risk.

And if mission fails, the whole thing fails.

What questions should I ask before starting?

The man who asks a question is a fool for a minute,
the man who does not ask is a fool for life.

Widely attributed to Confucius
(despite there being no evidence of his ever having said it).

It's a big decision to commit to becoming a director of a company, as it can have serious personal consequences. Directors of faith-based, not-for-profit corporations have the same legal responsibilities and potential liabilities as the directors of major public companies. In some very limited circumstances, directors can be held personally liable under the law for action that they take (or don't take) as board members. In extreme cases, if a court decides that a director has breached their directors' duties so badly that it amounts to dishonesty or gross negligence, it might even lead to criminal prosecution.

That's all pretty serious, and definitely best avoided. So before accepting a directorship of a company limited by guarantee (or any other company), you should check out the organisation by asking the right questions. These might include:

- What is the mission and purpose of the organisation?
    - You might think the answer is obvious ('well, it's a school!'), but this question is about the belief system behind the way the education is provided. The mission might be to focus on provision of education for vulnerable and disenfranchised students, or it might be to ensure excellence in education. These aims are not mutually exclusive, but the focus is different. Neither is right or wrong, but it's certainly beneficial if your own views align with the mission of the ministry.
    - Ask to see the foundational documents (Mission, Vision and Values statements). These should give you some insight into the nature of the organisation, although there is a bit of a risk of 'set and forget' when it comes to them.

- What is the relationship like between the board and the CEO?
  - This might feel like an impertinent question! But good relationships are absolutely key to good governance. How the board Chair (or the CEO) responds to that question might tell you a great deal about the organisation.
- Is the organisation in a strong financial position?
  - You are absolutely entitled to ask to see financial statements for, say, the last couple of years.
  - Do you see any evidence that the company is under financial pressure?
- What are the expectations of me as a board member?
  - How much time am I likely to need to commit each month?
    - How often are the meetings and how long do they usually run?
    - How much preparation time is generally required prior to meetings?
    - What other expectations does the board have of its directors?
  - Am I expected to be involved with fundraising? Or to attend fundraising events?
  - What ongoing support is provided to new board members?
  - Is there an induction process?
  - Is it expected that I will also join a subcommittee?
- Who is the governing body that the board reports to?
  - Ask to see the constitution. Amongst other things, the constitution sets out what powers are given to the board, as well as what powers are kept under the control of the member company (these are called reserve powers).
- What is the organisation's strategic outlook?
  - Ask to see their current strategic plan.

- What are the significant risks facing the organisation?
  - In not-for-profit ministries, funding is often one of the risks.
- Is there an up-to-date risk management framework?

You might come up with more.

In all your discussions, be conscious about how well the key people in the organisation relate to you and to others. Being able to relate well to people is essential to good governance.

You might feel awkward asking for all this information, particularly because the organisation is faith-based and you believe that it's undertaking good work. If the organisation is well governed and managed, you won't have any trouble getting the answers. Not only will this set your own mind at ease, but it will also give you clearer insight into the work that you are agreeing to become part of. What's more, it will show that you take your potential role as board director (and the responsibilities that go with it) seriously.

Will everyone be older/
younger/smarter
than me?

And, above all things, never think that you're not good enough yourself. (...) My belief is that in life people will take you very much at your own reckoning.

Anthony Trollope, *The Small House at Allington*

All sorts of people are on the boards of church-based ministries. I have served on boards with directors in their 80s and with directors in their 20s. Age, gender and sexual orientation are not barriers to becoming directors of church-based not-for-profits. Boards are (or should be) reflective of the communities with which they work.

There's every chance there will be people older than you on the board. Older people have two qualities that make them excellent board directors: experience and time. There's also every chance that there will be people younger than you on the board. Wisdom and experience are great, but a dynamic board also wants directors whose working knowledge is current.

One of the biggest barriers that can prevent people agreeing to come onto boards is the 'Impostor Syndrome'. I attended a very small regional secondary school. There were seven of us in my year 12 class. I spent most of my time as a student at Monash University, hoping that no-one would realise how much less I knew about pretty much everything than everyone else around me. When, many years later, I lectured in the Law School at Melbourne University, I realised how universal my experience had been. It didn't matter whether my students came from humble backgrounds or elite private schools: a surprising number of them at one time or another would seek out my private counsel on how to cope with the fact that everyone else in the group was smarter than them. (The other group – the students who knew they were the smartest in the room – rarely were.)

There might be people smarter than you on the board. Lucky you, if that's the case. I served on a board once with a religious sister who was in her 80s. She was a very sweet-looking old lady, and that sweetness sometimes lulled people into underestimating her. That was a mistake. She said very little in most board meetings (although she often smiled encouragingly at comments made by other directors). When she did speak, everyone stopped everything to focus on her. She was super smart. She would see a clear path through the mangroves when the rest of us were still hopelessly tangled. She was great at big picture vision but was also a details person. She had the most phenomenal memory and used it to remarkable effect.

Having really smart people on your board is very reassuring. It's also great to have really experienced people. And really sensible people. And shy people. And funny people. You get my point. A well-functioning board has a range of skills, talents, experience, backgrounds, and personality types.

The fact that you've been asked to join the ministry you've just joined (or that you're thinking of joining) means that *you* hold certain qualities that are needed on your board ministry. You might contribute industry expertise or lived experience or technical skill or relational ability or common sense and wisdom. The reason you've been invited onto the board is because you are the type of 'smart' that your ministry needs – now.

Are there risks involved in joining a board?

My only solution for the problem of habitual accidents ... is for everyone to stay in bed all day. Even then, there is always the chance that you will fall out.

Robert Benchley, *Chips off the Old Benchley.*

In 2016, I ran a risk-management seminar in Goroka, in the highlands of Papua New Guinea. There were about twenty Papua New Guinean attendees at the seminar, and they all worked for the ministry I was involved with. In groups, they had drawn on sheets of butchers paper a list of the risks they faced. They didn't make any distinction between risks that applied to them personally or the risks that affected their ministry. The four sheets of paper were taped up at the front of the room and, between them, they included the following suggestions:

- bad road condition
- violence (ethnic)
- drug addicts/mentally ill
- rascalism
- mothers bringing babies and children to training sessions
- roadblocks
- tribal fights
- empty promises
- street violence
- shortages of materials
- civil unrest
- danger during elections
- malnutrition
- access to health services
- high child and maternal mortality rates.

Four of the attendees came from Kiunga, where the primary form of travel is boat or plane. That group discussed the risk presented by the crocodiles living in the rivers they had to cross to reach the people they were providing services for, and whether it would be worthwhile spending money on lifesaver vests for the canoes. A significant part of that group's work was supporting asylum seekers and refugees who crossed the Fly River from West Papua to Kiunga. The man who ran the Kiunga office had himself been a West Papuan refugee years earlier. Asylum seekers risked being shot at and landing in the water with the crocodiles.

Yes, there are risks involved in joining a board. But everything's relative.

Potential board directors would be smart to ask the right questions about the company's operations before signing onto a directorship.[1] There are two types of risk for you to consider:

1. Your personal risk

Limited Liability

Under the law, directors of both **incorporated associations** and **companies limited by guarantee** have limited liability. This means that a company director's personal liability is limited to any fees that they may owe the organisation. Directors are not liable for debts that are incurred by the company (except in very limited circumstances that might include breach of fiduciary duties).[2]

Unincorporated associations are not recognised as separate legal entities. They cannot own property or enter contracts. An unincorporated association is simply a group of people who decide to form a committee for a common goal. For that reason, they are cheap and easy to create. Lots of sporting associations, for example, are unincorporated associations. They might be a small local group, or they might be a large national organisation.

As they are not a legal entity, committee members can potentially be personally liable for any contracts they sign and could potentially risk personal liability for civil claims that might be made against them, in their role as committee member.

Advisory board members (as the name implies) are advisors to the owner of the ministry and not decision makers. They are, therefore, not liable for losses incurred by the owner.

2. Ministry Risk

Risk management framework

As a board director, one of your important jobs will be to consider how much risk is the right amount for your board to take on, on behalf of the organisation. No business or organisation or individual or family can function without risk. Without it, there's no moving forward. Risk management is not about eradicating risk but about determining what level of risk you are prepared to accept and establishing a framework to manage that. As I discovered in Papua New Guinea, risk appetite varies wildly between organisations, depending on the circumstances they're in.

Some of the big questions we need to think about as a board are:

- How much risk we can live with, or what is our risk tolerance?
- What are our major risk categories? For example:
  - cyber security
  - reputational risk
  - finance
  - compliance
  - operational.
- What are the risks that fit within each of those categories?
- Do we have criteria in place to guide our decision making?
- What is the interplay between mission and our tolerance for risk exposure?

- Is our risk management process flexible enough to recognise and account for new and unexpected risks?
- Is our risk analysis big picture, accessible and not drowning in minutiae?

When it comes to risk, your role as a board member is not only to ensure that a risk management plan appropriate to your ministry is in place. If you are concerned about actions that the organisation is taking at either operational or board level and you think those actions leave the ministry open to significant risk, you need to speak up!

Let's say a group of people who have recently been involved with your ministry (we'll make it family members of aged-care home residents) make very unfavourable public comments about your CEO. Your board Chair calls an emergency meeting and shows you a letter that she's drafted, intending to send it to the families of all current residents. You think that the letter is aggressive and will only inflame the situation, and that it's likely to be leaked to the press.

You think it's important for the board (or some board representatives) to meet with the unhappy families and listen to exactly what their concerns are before any substantive response is made to their public comments. You also wonder whether the board should be seeking any advice, such as legal, communications or human resources advice, before attending the meeting. It's not your area of expertise and you're not sure exactly what advice the board might need, but you can see that the board might be at risk of reputational damage from this incident and that such damage could also lead to financial risk for the organisation. How does your mission impact on your response? To remain consistent with your mission statement and goals, what is your responsibility to the families and to the residents?

If no-one else on the board asks the questions that need asking – it's up to you! You're the one at the table.

Some ministries require very detailed risk-management plans, and others require much simpler frameworks. Risk management can be complex. This chapter gives a general indication of the way in which the question of risk impacts your decision-making as a board. It is not a 'how to' of risk management. There are lots of resources available to assist boards in finding and implementing a framework that's appropriate to the individual organisation.

Why is the terminology so confusing?

For I am a Bear of Very Little Brain, and long words Bother me.

A.A.Milne, *Winnie the Pooh*

Are you becoming a director of a company, or a ministry? Are you a board member or a board director? Who *are* the 'members', and what do they have to do with the owners of the company? Is the member of your ministry an MPJP or a PJP? Is your organisation run by a CEO, an Executive Director or someone else?

I'm not going to pretend that the terminology relating to faith-based organisations is consistent or sensible. The best I can do is provide some guidance. These are some of the things I found confusing when I started on the faith-based not-for-profit path.

Members vs Owners

- The members of a faith-based not-for-profit company are the owners of the company. They are the equivalent of shareholders in a for-profit company. Think of the terms 'members' and 'owners' interchangeably.
- Board directors are sometimes referred to as board members, which just creates confusion!
- In faith-based ministries, the members (or owners) of the company are likely to be either religious Orders, dioceses or Ministerial Public Juridic Persons[1].
- The members create the constitution, which (amongst other things):
    - defines the role/responsibilities of the company directors
    - defines the object or purpose of the company

- establishes the reserve powers – which are those powers which are retained by the members rather than being given to the directors. These might include the power to:
  - appoint (and remove) directors
  - amend the constitution
  - sell/acquire ministry property.

Some company members will have many ministries under their care, while others will have only one or two.

The member's liability (the amount that they are personally liable for in relation to the company) is limited to the amount that they guarantee upon registration of the company, which is always a nominal amount (often around $100).

Company vs ministry

If your board is an incorporated board[2], these words are interchangeable. Faith-based companies are often referred to as 'ministries' rather than 'companies'. There is no magic in the word 'ministry', other than the implication of outreach and care for others, in ways that we don't usually associate with the word 'company'.

Not-for-profit vs For purpose

Not-for-profit organisations are now sometimes referred to as 'for purpose' organisations. The difference is purely philosophical in some cases, and in others is a bit more nuanced. No business can run without a profit, including a 'not-for-profit'. To meet the criteria required to claim the tax benefits of a charity, a not-for-profit *can* make a profit but must only use that profit for the purposes of the organisation. 'For purpose' organisations acknowledge the need for all organisations to make a profit; they consider 'for purpose'

a more accurate representation of the work they do. It is also an acknowledgement for many organisations, that the profit made by one sector subsidises the losses that might be incurred in other, more mission-based, sectors.

CEO vs Executive Director

Again, there is no magic in the title of the leader of your ministry. Traditionally, CEO (Chief Executive Officer) tended to apply to leaders of for-profit companies, while Executive Director was more common in not-for-profits. This is a very flexible landscape though, and there are many CEOs of not-for-profits.

In not-for-profits, the CEO or Executive Director is not usually a voting member of the board. They lead the operational arm of the ministry and are employed by the board. They attend board meetings and report to the board on operational management. While they do not have voting rights, their input to meetings is essential, as they are the person who knows the most about the organisation.

It is good governance for the board to have an in camera session, namely time spent without the Executive Director or other staff, at the end of board meetings. These meetings give the board the opportunity for confidential discussion about a range of issues, including the performance of the Executive Director, without the presence of operational staff. There are different views on whether in camera sessions should be held after each meeting or only occasionally, and good reason to do it either way. My personal view is that it's better to have them after each meeting so that it becomes routine. That way, your Executive Director (and any other staff in attendance) are less likely to be stricken with fear at the unusual announcement that an in camera session has been called! Most of these meetings are short and nothing of particular importance is canvassed. However, it gives all board directors a regular opportunity to raise any concerns, particularly if they are unsure whether their concern is a sensitive matter or not.

MPJP vs PJP

An MPJP or Ministerial Public Juridic Person, is a relatively new form of governance structure within the Catholic church. MPJPs are incorporated entities which are the members of many Catholic not-for-profit ministries.[3] Just to make matters more confusing, for historical reasons, they are often referred to as PJPs, with the 'ministerial' part of MPJP left off altogether. For our purposes, you can consider them as the same thing.

ASIC vs ACNC

The Australian Securities and Investment Commission, or **ASIC**, is an independent body to which the Australian federal government has given the task of regulating Australian companies (as well as financial services). The Australian Charities and Not-for-profits Commission or **ACNC**, was also established as an independent body by the federal government. Its role is to regulate charities and not-for-profit organisations in Australia. Your ministry will be required to comply with regulatory requirements imposed by these bodies.

What if I can't stand another board member?

I have been bent and broken but – I hope – into better shape.

Charles Dickens, *Great Expectations*

Productive relationships are central to good governance. So, the day that both the Executive Director and the Chair of the finance committee threatened to resign wasn't a good governance day for me. I had been board Chair of that particular faith-based ministry for about four months.

Discussion during the previous evening's board meeting had been 'robust'. Robust discussion is OK. In fact, robust discussion is desirable for a board. Arguably, that's the director's role: to be an active, independent and engaged participant in discussion. Being aggressive and offensive, however, is not desirable or part of the role, and that was the allegation that was made against the new finance committee chair at the end of the meeting. I had missed the danger signs.

I have a background as a mediator, and in mediation it's essential that all parties speak the same language. Not just the same spoken language, but cultural differences, religious differences, ethnic differences can all result in different parties using familiar words with each other but meaning quite different things by them. One person's 'compromise' is another's 'capitulation'. One person's 'we like to be inclusive' is another's 'they're so demanding'.

In this case, the new finance committee chair was a senior director of an international accounting firm by day and had become a volunteer director of our not-for-profit by night (and by day as well, actually). He was accustomed to meetings that were brief and direct, and his language reflected that. By way of contrast, our Executive Director led this church-based organisation that was firmly based in a mission of care and support for the individual. (It was, of course, a desire to support that very mission that had attracted our accountant to his new role). Within the ministry, every morning started with a time of prayer and reflection before the work of the day began.

The accountant's comments were forthright. They were not personalised – well at least not to his mind, or to mine. He did what very large organisations paid him a great deal of money to do, which was to point out our systemic organisational weaknesses. As I listened, I felt gratitude and relief that we had acquired this man's expertise. For some others, however, and for our Executive Director in particular, the experience was humiliating. I did not take steps to 'pull in' the accountant during the meeting, because I didn't pick up on the intense hurt felt by the Executive Director until the meeting was closed – when shaken, he told me he felt it to be a personal attack. My own apologies and reassurances did not dispel his deep hurt.

We had a clash of cultures.

The following day, I contacted the accountant to explain what had happened. His first response was to eye roll (we were speaking on the phone, but I could feel it), and tell me that if there were individuals who couldn't hear the truth, he didn't have the time to waste on them, and it was probably better for him to resign and give us the chance to find someone else who'd be a better fit for the role.

I subsequently had a call from the Executive Director. He told me that he'd spent the night going over what had happened, and he thought that as it seemed the board had lost faith in him, he should probably resign and give us the chance to find someone else who'd be a better fit for the role.

I knew:

1. The Executive Director was skilled, professional, and entirely capable of listening to and accepting constructive criticism. This incident had not felt like constructive criticism to him, but like an attack.
2. The accountant had not intended to attack anyone. He intended to provide valuable feedback to the organisation to improve its operation. (His 'valuable feedback' was the Executive Director's 'attack'.)
3. The accountant delivered his report without considering that it was a group of committed, mission-based employees and volunteers that he was addressing, and not well-paid directors of a large publicly listed for-profit company.

4. I had inadvertently let the meeting run out of control.

The problem was not the information given, but the way it was delivered. To bridge the communication gap:

1. The Executive Director, the accountant and I all took the time to sit with, listen to and understand each other.
2. We all agreed to modify behaviour to meet the needs of the other.
3. Time was set aside in our next board meeting for the whole board to address any remaining concerns.

At the end of the process, we knew that whenever significant differences of opinion occurred in the future (as we all knew they would), those differences would be discussed in an honest, transparent and respectful way. I can honestly say that the quality of communication between all board members was vastly improved as a result. We became far more of a team.

In mediation, the prospects of a successful outcome are exponentially increased when all the parties involved share a common end goal. That was the case with this board. We had common values and a shared vision for the future of the organisation. We needed time to talk through (separately and together and over time) the differences that were in the way. And we did.

Often board directors become friends over time. But it's not necessary that they do. It's not even necessary that they particularly like each other. They do, however, need to be respectful, and able to communicate very effectively. Energy put into working on respectful and transparent communication is extremely worthwhile. Building trust results in productive relationships. And productive relationships are at the heart of good governance.

13

What do
Subcommittees do?

'You know everything has to be examined and voted on by the committee,' said the cautious Secretary.

Oliver Wendell Holmes Sr, *A Mortal Anthipathy*

A lot of the work of a board gets done by committees, which in not-for-profits are often referred to as subcommittees (the board itself being the 'committee' implied in 'subcommittee'). These committees are often made up of a mix of board directors, and non-directors. Subcommittees have a specialised area of focus, and they make recommendations to the board.

For example, most company boards (even small ones) will have a subcommittee which might be called the finance committee or the audit committee or the finance, risk and audit committee, depending on the particular role given to that committee by the board. The committee is governed by a charter which has been approved by the board. The charter is usually a simple document, setting out the role and purpose of the subcommittee and the rules it is bound by.

The finance risk and audit committee, for example, under the leadership of the Chair of that committee, works with the business manager to prepare the budget, considers investment options, oversees the risk management framework, and ensures compliance with audit requirements. (Most companies are required to appoint external auditors to annually review their financial statements to ensure that they are accurate and compliant with relevant legislation).

Subcommittees do not make governance decisions but make recommendations to the board. It's the board that makes the decisions. For example, the budget will be workshopped within the finance subcommittee until that committee is satisfied with it, and it is then put to the board with a recommendation for approval. All board directors must have the opportunity to consider the proposed budget, and the chance to pose questions or request adjustments. When it comes to audit time, the subcommittee chair is likely to have liaised with the auditors during the audit process, but it's the board that has an *in camera* meeting with the auditor prior to finalisation of the financial reports. This is an opportunity for the auditor to speak frankly to the directors without the CEO, the business manager, or other staff or company officers present.

Subcommittees are sometimes referred to as the 'engine room of the board'. The heart of the board's work happens in subcommittees, and it's worthwhile investing the time to ensure that the subcommittees you have are the right ones for your organisation, and that they have the right members for their task.

Subcommittees are often made up of a combination of board directors and non-board directors. Often, boards have power under their constitution to appoint subcommittee members without the approval of the members (unlike the appointment of board directors, which is usually a power reserved by the members).

There are excellent reasons for appointing non-board directors to subcommittees. It gives the board the opportunity to engage people with skills or experience beyond those of the board members. Being on a subcommittee might appeal to people who would like to contribute to the ministry, but who do not have the time to commit to becoming a director. It can also be a great way for both the board and the non-board subcommittee members to test each other out for possible board inclusion in the future.

While much of the board's work is done by the various subcommittees, it doesn't follow that the more subcommittees you have, the more work gets done! It's important to bear in mind that having lots of subcommittees in a small ministry doesn't equal good governance. There are several reasons for this:

1. Subcommittees all need to be filled with people. In a small ministry, that means spreading your board directors thinly.
2. You need to have at least one or two people who will be attending all the subcommittee meetings, or you run a real risk of the left hand not knowing what the right hand is doing. Committees are a bit like boiling pots: lots of interesting stuff goes on in them, but the valuable ideas and discussion tend to evaporate in the process of preparing the committee minutes that will got to the board.

3. Non-director committee members will need to be appointed. This is necessary for the committees to have the depth of experience and wisdom necessary for good decision-making. As mentioned above, this can be a way for new people to become involved in the ministry, and to give both them and the board a chance to try each other out before any possible future appointment to the board. People with the appropriate skills to step into these roles can be hard to find. It follows that the more committees you have, the more time you'll spend looking for committee members.

Some subcommittees will meet frequently while others might only meet a few times a year. Like the board, they should be driven by the mission of the organisation, and work with the timetable of the organisation and the board. Your meetings should have a purpose: directors are busy and generous people and shouldn't be subjected to meetings for meetings' sake. For example, if you are a small ministry that sometimes provides grants to third parties, it might only be necessary for the grants subcommittee to meet at application time each year, and at reporting time. Of course, those meetings should always take place a week or two before a board meeting, so that any recommendations made by the subcommittee can be dealt with expeditiously by the board.

Some organisations will have lots of subcommittees, and others very few. What's right for you will depend on the nature of your organisation. What matters is that you are thoughtful about getting the balance right.

14

Am I the only one feeling confused?

'Really now you ask me,' said Alice, very much confused, 'I don't think—'

'Then you shouldn't talk,' said the Hatter.

Lewis Carroll, *Alice's Adventures in Wonderland*

When I was first appointed to a board as a director, I spent the first few meetings feeling confused. I understood the theory that the board was the body that set strategy and direction; I also understood, or thought I understood, the importance of being an active participant in decision-making rather than a passive observer. I understood that my role carried significant legal responsibility, and I took that seriously.

What I didn't understand was when or where the discussion about strategy and direction happened. I also didn't understand when I was going to get the opportunity to be an active participant in decision-making that was above the lowest, every-day level. I felt genuinely confused about our rolling agendas, which barely needed to be updated from one meeting to the next. We had our meetings, discussed more or less the same matters in the same order and approved all the resolutions each time, because there was never anything significant to decide on.

I did not have practical experience in the business of the organisation. I had been brought onto the board largely because of my legal background. I had also expressed views about future strategy, which fitted with the views of the members who appointed me. But none, or at least far too few, of those strategic discussions ever seemed to happen at our board table. For some time, I sat wondering what on earth was going on. I was a first-time director and didn't have the experience to understand exactly what I was missing, but I knew that I was missing something. Where were all the discussions about the big issues, such as thoughts about future direction, and details about risks attaching to existing contracts? I can now say that I was confused about who was governing the business, and when that governing was happening. Because it didn't seem to be happening at the board table.

You might wonder how important matters can be kept from an active and engaged board. Think about Donald Rumsfeld's 'unknown unknowns'.

You don't know what you don't know, and so as a director, it can be hard to find the right questions to ask. As a new director you can also feel a bit foolish. If the other directors don't seem to be concerned about the flow of information, you might presume that you are missing something that everyone else has understood.

Being left in the dark as a director is often the result of a traditional form of governance, known as 'the backroom chat'. This seemed to be the way that much of the business of my first board came about. These backroom chats are counter-productive to genuinely transparent governance. I'm not talking about bouncing ideas off another board director or seeking input from a director with specialist knowledge prior to a meeting; this is all about effectively making the big decisions away from the board table.

Part of the discernment process of decision-making is the process of collegiate group discussion – and that process is undermined if slabs of the discussion take place away from most of the board directors. Further, if those slabs of private discussion consistently translate into actual decision-making away from the board table, that's a significant governance failure.

Ask your questions – even if you're not entirely sure about which questions you want to ask. Get your concerns onto the board table so that the discussion can start. You might find that the answers are quick and straightforward, or you might find that far from being the only person at the table feeling confused, you are one of many. It's not only sensible to do your best to resolve the confusion, but it's your responsibility as a director.

Should I join
if the organisation
is a bit run down?

I like the dreams of the future better than the history of the past.

Thomas Jefferson, *Letter to John Adams* (1861)

A friend contacted me recently and said she'd joined the board of an incorporated, church owned, not-for-profit. She'd been a bit involved with the organisation when she was a university student but had not had anything to do with it in the subsequent 20 years or so. She agreed to become a director primarily because of the fond memories she still carried of her earlier days with them.

She had attended three board meetings by the time she was speaking to me. She felt that she was still finding her way around the organisation. She hadn't seen the constitution or the financial reports prior to agreeing to join, and after the three meetings she felt unclear about what the mission of the ministry was.

She was concerned that:

- While the purpose of the ministry was to provide grants to third parties, there was significant disagreement within the board about what types of third parties it should fund. Discussion on this issue at the board meetings had moved from 'robust' into 'directors screaming at each other'.
- The grants that the ministry made came from interest payments received on a corpus of cash that had been invested some years earlier. Over recent times, the grants had sometimes been made from the corpus, as well as from the interest.
- The ministry was entitled to access the corpus to make the grants, but doing so meant that the invested funds were eroding, and the interest earned was dwindling.
- The business could not remain viable for more than another 3–4 years if that funding model continued.

Was it time for her to resign and run?

My answer was a definitive 'maybe', and we discussed the following:

1. She needed to be absolutely sure that the company was still solvent. Directors who allow a company to continue to incur debt when it is insolvent, are at risk of becoming personally liable for those debts.[1]
2. If the company was still solvent, then the board had options:
    a. It could look at whether there were new ways to grow income and continue the ministry.

    or

    b. If the board felt that the time had come to close the organisation, they could work toward doing so in an efficient and productive way that would hopefully enable recognition of its achievements over the years.
3. Either way, the board needed to be in agreement about their current purpose.
4. Given the level of dissent, I suggested that an external facilitator might be helpful in assisting the board to revisit their mission and strategic purpose at this crucial point of their existence.

To be a director on this board in the next few years would require significant commitment. Major strategic decisions would need to be made that will have a major impact on the operation of the ministry.

So, to stay or to run?

On the one hand:

- If my friend believed that it was possible to bring the board together on mission (with or without the assistance of a facilitator) *and* if she felt that the mission was sufficiently important to her

to commit to, then she should see the process through. Time – and information provided to the board – would tell whether that process would enable the ministry to continue, or whether that process would turn out to be the orderly winding down of the business so that it finished well.

On the other hand:

- If she did not see any realistic hope of the board reaching agreement on mission *or* if she did not have any particular interest in what that mission might end up being, then she would probably be better off cutting her losses and resigning.

A messy board-realignment process can be a positive thing, provided it has directors who are prepared to commit the necessary time and energy. With faith based not-for-profits, the motivation is generally a deep commitment to the mission of the organisation. If you have that commitment, you might decide that it's worth dedicating the time that will be needed. Without such a commitment, you're probably better off bowing out gracefully.

16

How much time
will it take?

Time travels in divers paces with divers persons.

Shakespeare, *As you like it*

This is a tough one to answer. It's a classic, 'how long *is* that piece of string?'

As a generalisation, board meetings for faith-based ministries such as schools and community services, were traditionally held once a month or so, and each meeting probably went for two or three hours. Increasingly, this model is changing to suit individual needs. Meetings might be held on a regular basis (every month or second month) or they might be diarised around the work of the organisation (the times that approvals are needed for applications, or budget time, or the compliance schedule etc.).

The board papers should always be sent out to board members at least one week prior to the meeting, and while the time you will need to prepare will vary from board to board, you will probably need at least two or three hours.

That's it for your core commitment. However, there's every chance you'll be asked to sit on a board subcommittee such as a finance, risk and audit committee or governance committee or strategic planning committee or succession committee or any number of other committees. That means an extra meeting on top of the board meeting, and it also means engaging in the work of that subcommittee. How much work that will entail varies according to the needs of the task and your own commitment to it.

You will need to discuss the expectations on you as a subcommittee member with the Chair of that committee before you join. Depending on the nature of the subcommittee, it might meet as often as the board does, or it might have only two or three meetings a year. Subcommittee meetings are generally held a week or two before board meetings so that resolutions made by the committee can be put to the board for discussion and voting.

Even if you're not on a subcommittee, you might on occasion be called to join a small, short-term advisory group. This might be for a specific task that is likely to require a couple of meetings and/or phone calls and perhaps some research. (Should you get some insight into the current property market to help decide whether to sell (or buy) that building? Do you need a new subcommittee? Can you contact your network and put feelers out for possible new board members?) Or, if you have skills that are particularly relevant to an issue that is affecting the organisation at a point in time, you might be asked to provide guidance and support to the CEO or senior staff. (Has there been some bad publicity? Are new policies urgently needed?) It's important to note that 'providing guidance and support' doesn't mean 'stepping into the shoes of'!

Directors are the *governors* of the business, not the *operators* of it.

As a director, you might have occasional conversations between meetings with other directors and/or the board Chair, but your time commitment is largely limited to meetings and preparation time. You are likely to need to attend site visits relevant to your ministry, particularly early in your time as a director. This might also be a regular event for your board, as a means of keeping you connected to the 'on the ground' operation of the ministry.

Being board Chair is another story entirely! While leading an organisation can be immensely stimulating and satisfying, it also requires the time commitment of a part-time job.

Finally, the Covid-19 pandemic has familiarised us all with the flexibility that video-sharing platforms can offer. I once chaired a national faith-based ministry, where the directors all flew to Sydney for each of our meetings. Allowing directors, particularly volunteer directors, the flexibility of sometimes attending meetings from work or home for a couple of hours rather than having to take a whole day to attend in person, is hugely beneficial. It might also increase the pool of directors available for your board. We shouldn't forget though, that nothing replaces the human experience of being physically present with each other, and the creativity that sparks when we are.

Do I need to be a parent to be on a school board?

(Or do I need to have medical training to be on a hospital board…or do I need to live with a disability to be on a disability support board?)

It is like a barber's chair, that fits all buttocks…

Shakespeare, *All's well that ends well*

No.

The fact that lots of school boards have lots of parents on them is absolutely *not* because it's essential to be a parent at the school to have anything worthwhile to offer the school board. School boards, understandably, have parents on them because it's good to have a range of people on the board who are invested in the decisions that the board makes, and parents are certainly invested. They are the easiest group to motivate into action.

However, having too many parents of current students on a school board is not particularly healthy for the board. The board makes decisions that will impact the direction of the school for years to come, and sometimes that causes a conflict of interest for parents of current or future students. 'The new master plan sounds great, but can we delay the commencement of the building works until my kids are finished at the school'? 'Or perhaps can we expedite the works to get them finished before my kids start?'.

Like any board, a school board should have representation from various stakeholder groups. For example, recently graduated students can provide insight into contemporary education that no-one else on the board, including the principal, will have. School boards also need professional expertise: directors with experience in public relations, finance, accounting and investment, governance, faith and mission, human relations, legal systems and many other types of professional expertise.

Often previous students from the school are approached to contribute this expertise. Having a personal connection with the school is the usual impetus for committing to becoming a director, but it needn't be. Perhaps your neighbours' children went to the school, and you were impressed by the school's emphasis on social justice. Or perhaps you are inspired by the school's commitment to supporting non-mainstream students through its creative arts program. It is more important that you understand and respect the culture and mission of the school, than that you have any direct personal connection with it.

Diversity on boards is, in fact, essential for effective governance. Gender and ethnic diversity should be a given, but this remains a work in progress for many boards. Boards should reflect the community. Are you working with an at-risk community, such as people living with autism? Do you have those people on your board? Do you have their parents? Their employers? Their carers? Are you working with communities from developing countries? Do you have people from those communities on your board?

It can be really hard to achieve this kind of diversity. It's hard to find people who are prepared to take on the role, and who have the skills necessary to do so. Would paying board members increase the potential pool of directors?[1] We can't have every single potential stakeholder represented or the board would be unworkable. But we do need to strive toward greater diversity. Not so long ago, faith-based boards were almost exclusively made up of middle-aged white men who made all the decisions about helping the groups they worked with. That sounds like a criticism, but in fact it's not. It was the way of the world then, and they were mostly highly capable men who generously volunteered their time to help others and who made a positive difference to people's lives. My father was amongst that group. Today we seek to work alongside our partner groups as equals, rather than being their 'helpers'. Having the voice of our partner groups on our boards, while sometimes tough to achieve, is not only valuable, but necessary.

18

How do I find out
what's going on?

I only ask for information.

Charles Dickens, *David Copperfield*

You've been told in your board induction process that it's not your role to run the business, because running the business is the role of the Executive Director. It's a bit like, 'You're governance, they're operations, and what happens in operations stays in operations.' You can't approach staff members about their performance because that's operational, and therefore a matter for the Executive Director. You can't just decide to put on a training session for the staff, because staff professional development is operational, and therefore a matter for the Executive Director.

Your role is not to manage the day-to-day operations, but to ensure, through the establishment and maintenance of strong governance structures and processes, that the Executive Director:

- efficiently and effectively achieves ministry objectives by implementing the strategic plan
- establishes effective relationships with staff and stakeholders (such as partners and donors)
- complies with external and internal regulatory requirements and
- ensures that mission is imbedded throughout the organisation.

All well and good. But then, how on earth do you know what's going on?

1. Reports

At each board meeting, you will receive detailed reports from the Executive Director as well as from the Chairs of each of the committees. The committees look in detail at different aspects of the operation and/or governance of the business. The finance, audit and risk committee for example, will provide detailed feedback on how the organisation has been performing financially since the previous board meeting, and will provide appropriate comparator data. Are you in a better or worse financial position than you were this time last year? If there's a significant difference in either direction – why?

The Executive Director's report gives you a snapshot of what has been going on in the ministry since the last board meeting. They report on what's happening in the business – which should include the good, the bad and the ugly. They'll tell you who they've had important meetings with, or why a highly valued staff member resigned, or why the staff are keen to commence work on a new project. Board directors then have the opportunity to ask questions or raise concerns.

2. Board Guests

A great way for board directors to get further insight into the 'on the ground' work of the ministry, is to regularly allow time in the agenda for guest speakers at board meetings. Having staff members, ministry partners (the beneficiaries of ministry activity), volunteers and other stakeholders regularly give short presentations to the board is a very effective way of giving directors insight into the ministry that they are governing. It also gives directors the opportunity to ask questions of people they don't normally have access to. It helps keep directors engaged in their work, because without ongoing contact with the actual business of the ministry, there is a risk of directors becoming disengaged from the work itself.

The presentations need only be quite short – 10 minutes or so. If they are any longer, they become difficult to fit into a crowded agenda; it's all too easy to drop them to allow for the 'essentials' such as finance, compliance, and risk. But board engagement with and understanding of the work is essential too. Hearing from the people involved in the heart of the business is more likely to happen if the presentations are short and regular rather than long, detailed, and infrequent.

3. Allowing time to gather together

A couple of times a year, it's great if board members and staff can spend informal time together. How feasible this is will obviously depend on the size of the ministry and other matters. Boards can sometimes take on almost mythical properties in the eyes of the staff because board directors are not 'on the ground', so it's humanising for both staff and board directors to have this opportunity. Relaxed, informal conversations provide insight and hopefully understanding of the other's role. Site visits can be a great opportunity for achieving this kind of connectivity.

Good governance is relational.

19

Do I have to agree
with everyone else?

Quoting again from experience, a new birth, a change of heart, is perfectly possible…
M.K. Gandhi, *Third Class in Indian Railways*

Robust discussion between board members is healthy. For that reason, having people on boards who have different views and outlooks is healthy. Difference is invigorating – or it should be – for board members. Managing different views in board meetings can be challenging for the Chair, but it's also what gives the board the impetus to move forward. Tempting as it might be to put together a board of like-minded directors, it means that you lose the creative spark that's lit by respectful and constructive disagreement.

What does that mean?

Let's say that you think that your social media campaign manager targeted your recent campaign to the wrong audience. You believe that fewer donations have come in as a result, and this has impacted on the number of people that your ministry has been able to support. You see this as a symptom of bigger problems in your communications department. You know that managing the performance of the social media campaign manager is an operational matter, and therefore a matter for the Executive Director, but you think that the issue is important enough for the board to revisit the strategic plan in relation to communications, and this is the suggestion you make. The other board members acknowledge your concerns but vote down your suggestion for a review because they say that other matters have higher priority.

Or what if, because of a significant fall in funds, the CEO raises the option of accepting donations from a mining company, despite the mission of your organisation being partly based in environmental sustainability?

The first scenario is about how your operational objective (increased fundraising) is achieved. The second is about how to improve fundraising as well, but it is also about your mission or purpose (environmental sustainability). To an extent, disagreement about *how* your board goes about achieving what it sets out to achieve, is what you are there on the board to do! Fresh eyes and fresh ideas are healthy for a board's growth, and a good board chair encourages constructive discussion of alternative viewpoints. When it comes to the 'what', however, what your mission or purpose is – there should be clarity within the board. Board formation and ongoing development should help to ensure that board directors remain clear and consistent in their views about what the organisation is there to achieve.

This might sound obvious, but there are a surprising number of boards out there that are not clear about that simple issue of 'what are we here to do?' and it leaves the board vulnerable to ongoing friction.

It's absolutely fine for you to disagree with everyone else about an important decision. Disagreement helps to inoculate a board against complacency. You should have the opportunity to have your views heard, provided you do so respectfully and constructively. You should also be listened to respectfully and constructively. If you find yourself in the minority, you will need to be able to accept the majority decision gracefully.

Board decision-making will not usually require unanimity. You might find yourself constantly in the minority view in a way that is constructive and healthy for the board and that's a great position to be in. You might even find that other board members actively look to you to provide alternative viewpoints.

If a pattern of non-constructive disagreement looks like becoming entrenched, however, you should consider discussing your concerns with the board Chair. Sometimes the air might need to be cleared between individuals, and a good board Chair should be adept at facilitating effective communication. You are all on the board to serve a common goal, and in all but extreme cases it's likely that communication difficulties will be manageable, although occasionally, skilled external support might be required to reach that point.

The extreme end of disagreement might require more drastic action. Perpetual, enmeshed, negative disagreement is life-sapping for everyone. If all the collaborative work you do with the Chair and other directors to address the conflict fails to lead to more effective and productive communication, it may not be in your own interests or the interest of the organisation for you to remain on the board.

Finally, if you consider the direction that the board is taking to be not just misguided, but ethically, morally or legally wrong to the extent that you believe you cannot continue to fulfil your fiduciary duty, then the appropriate response is for you to table your objections to the board, ensure that your concerns are minuted, and resign.

20

What is a fiduciary duty?

There is one thing, Emma, which a man can always do if he chooses, and that is, his duty; not by manoeuvring and finessing, but by vigour and resolution.

Jane Austen, *Emma*

A fiduciary duty is a duty to act with care, diligence and undivided loyalty toward the ministry or organisation of which you are a director, over and above any other interest, including personal interest.

Ways of breaching your fiduciary duty include:

- allowing the ministry to continue trading while insolvent
- engaging in decision-making, despite a conflict of interest
- obtaining information dishonestly
- using ministry information for personal gain
- providing confidential ministry information to third parties, whether you personally gain from doing so or not.

One of your most important duties is to ensure that the company doesn't trade while insolvent – meaning that it is unable to pay its debts when they are due. If you have grounds to be concerned that this might be happening, the board must either satisfy itself that the company does in fact have the funds to meet its debts or it *must* take action to cease trading.

Directors must also notify the board of any matters in relation to which they might have a conflict of interest. For example, if the board is considering employing a consultant to provide expert advice to the board on a particular issue, and one of the nominees for the role is a close relative of a board member, the board member has a duty to refrain from engaging in both the discussion and the decision about their employment. Your loyalty as director is to the ministry and not to yourself or your relative.

It's important that you understand that the work you undertake together as a board is confidential. In not-for-profit organisations, it's perhaps not uncommon for board directors to know and be friends with staff members.

That friendship might even be what led you to your role as director. Of course, you can maintain your friendship while you are a director, but you cannot reveal confidential board discussion to non-board members.

Directors of church based not-for-profits have the same responsibilities and potential liabilities as the directors of public companies under the *Corporations Act*, 2001 (Cth). Directors can be held personally liable under statute and common law if they breach their fiduciary duty to the organisation. A breach of fiduciary duty might even lead to criminal prosecution if the court finds that the breach amounts to dishonesty on the part of the director.

That sounds intimidating, and it should. However, all it really means is that you need to take your role as director seriously. For that reason, make sure that you:

- understand the board papers
- can be confident that the company is solvent
- have all the information you need to make informed decisions.
- ask questions or ask for further information if you need to, from the Executive Director, the board Chair or the relevant subcommittee Chair.

It is not enough for you to rely on the recommendation of another board director. It's important that you take the time to understand the issues and the likely consequences of the decisions you make as director.

You have a fiduciary duty to do so.

21

What is 'formation'?

... I will light in your heart the lamp of understanding, which shall not be put out ...

Apocrypha, 2 Esdras 14.25, NRSV Bible

Formation is the process of being 'formed' in the tradition and culture of an organisation. People entering religious orders are 'formed' in the tradition of that order. It's a type of spiritual and educational training. As lay people coming onto church-based boards, we go through a process of being formed in both the tradition and culture of the organisation we are joining, as well as the tradition and culture of the member organisation that created it.

The idea of formation can sound a bit off-putting to potential board members who are not particularly, or even at all, involved with the church. Formation is not evangelisation. It's not necessary for all board members to share the faith tradition of the ministry or its members, and you are not being asked to do that. Formation is learning *about* the tradition. Board members don't all need to share in that tradition, but they do need to understand it, be respectful of it, and above all, be supportive of the mission that has grown from it.

Liturgy and prayer are integral to many faith traditions and will be part of a church-based ministry formation experience. Typically, a board meeting might begin with a prayer or poem or reading, and some personal reflection time. This gives individual board directors the opportunity to remove themselves from whatever other pressures are impacting them and allow themselves the physical and mental space to focus on the mission of the ministry that has brought them to that table at that time. There is likely to be formation time at the start of your board meeting (perhaps 10-15 minutes), and there might occasionally be Board formation afternoons, or even days. In my experience, these days are looked forward to by board directors, as in our very hectic lives it's become almost an indulgence to allow time: time for silence, time for reflection and time for personal prayer.

Formation is likely to be rooted – either directly or indirectly – in Catholic Social Teaching (CST). CST is a body of principles concerned with the centrality of human dignity. It addresses issues such as oppression, inequality of wealth distribution and ecological injustice. The foundation for these principles has been drawn from scripture but they also encompass contemporary writing and thinking. CST is often defined as having seven principles, although different organisations might adapt them to have more or fewer than seven. CST is not static, but it is always grounded in enabling equality of hope and opportunity for all. The seven principles are often defined as:

- the life and dignity of the human person
- the common good
- subsidiarity (the opportunity for all people to participate in decisions that affect them)
- solidarity
- preferential option for the poor and vulnerable
- the dignity and rights of workers
- care for the earth.

These principles are the principles upon which many of our mission statements are based. More than that though, they are also a valuable aid in discernment (deep thought and reflection), when it comes to making difficult decisions. They are a touchpoint for maintaining integrity as a faith-based ministry, whose purpose is to support the dignity of all.

In 2021, the *Laudato Si'* Action Platform was launched by the Vatican. It is a program intended to assist ministries, communities and families to work toward 'full sustainability in the holistic spirit of integral ecology' (laudatosiactionplatform.org). The *Laudato Si'* Action Platform has 7 goals:

- response to the cry of the earth
- response to the cry of the poor
- ecological economics
- adoption of sustainable lifestyles
- ecological education

- ecological spirituality
- community resilience and empowerment.

The Action Platform fits neatly with CST, as a concrete way of applying some of the central dimensions of CST. While maintaining focus on human dignity, it also highlights the immediacy of the need for action to protect our earth.

Respect for human dignity and responsibility for care of the earth are not just philosophical concepts for our ministries. They should be central to our decision-making.

Regular formation is also a process for 'reality testing' that the mission of your organisation remains aligned with that of the members who created it. You might consider prevailing cultural norms within your organisation and discuss the ways in which they fit with your mission and the ways in which they don't.

Formation is one of the most significant means by which the members of the company ensure that your ministry's work and vision continues to live into the future. It is big-picture, and not operational. It's not about the nitty gritty of how work gets done, but about why it is done, and the philosophical and theological basis for it. New board members should attend a formation program prior to starting their tenure, or early in their term as a board director. But formation is not just part of an induction package. It's an essential ongoing process to check in on mission and to consider that most fundamental question: 'Why are we all here doing this?' Formation is not just for the board. The operational arm of the organisation will also need ongoing formation. Sometimes there might be joint gatherings of board and staff for that purpose.

Formation is part of mission governance. While board members might have many different views about the best way to achieve your ministry's mission goals, all board members need to be on the same page when it comes to the mission itself.

22

IS Strategic planning really boring?

One cannot have too large a party.

Jane Austen, *Emma*

One of the major responsibilities of a board is setting the strategic direction of the organisation it governs. This is the big-picture stuff. What plans do you have for the future of your ministry, and how do you plan to get there? In the simplest terms, approving the plan is the job of the board, and the staff then set about implementing it.

Strategic planning is done in conjunction with the Executive Director because they are the one responsible for rolling out the board's plan. Management will prepare the draft plan, which is then put to the board for input and eventual approval. Staff should be engaged in the process at appropriate stages, to provide input in relation to objectives, and to help reality-test proposals. Collaboration with staff helps ensure that your plan is achievable. It also invests them in the plan that they will ultimately implement.

Traditionally, board strategic planning days were held every 5 years or so. The mission and vision statements would be reviewed, and a new, forward-looking 5-year plan prepared, usually with the assistance of a facilitator. More recently, there has been a tendency to move away from the 5-year timetable, partly because projecting 5 years ahead seems increasingly unrealistic and, well, old school in such a rapidly changing environment. Boards are more likely to have smaller and more frequent strategy sessions, and to tweak plans as needed, rather than have infrequent major strategy-planning days.

Some of this will take place in board meetings, with time for consideration of strategic issues allowed for in the agenda. This time can be particularly useful for 'reality checking' mission: Does recent board decision-making fit within the umbrella of your ministry's mission? What processes do you have in place to ensure that continues to happen?

The new nimbleness makes sense. But sometimes you will need to take more time than can be allowed for in your regular meetings. Every now and again it is essential for boards to focus on big-picture strategy. This is not about realigning outcomes based on changed circumstances, but on reimagining and challenging assumptions. Big-picture planning is an opportunity to consider the unthinkable. Merger? New funding model? Pivot from domestic to international (or vice versa)? Throw the paint on the canvas.

The best strategic-planning day I have attended involved a huge number of people – not a strategy I'd recommend for all your planning days. It was a time for change management for the school I was involved with. The planning day was facilitated by Colin Pidd of Conversant Solutions, and he encouraged us to go big. We started off by listing all the groups who had an interest in the ministry, and we invited most of them to join us (or representative groups of them anyway): board members, staff (professional and administrative), students, parents, old girls and even neighbours. It was a big unruly bunch, who all loved the school and wanted to see it continue to thrive into the future. It was a day of looking back at the best things about where we had come from, of reflection about where we were, and a day of imagining what we might become: opportunities for community involvement, master-planning dreaming, environmental opportunities, social justice outreach, the practical and the unobtainable were all on the table (on lots of tables, actually – there were a lot of people, so there was a lot of small group work).

Lots of butchers paper was used, but by no means wasted. Over time, lists of all kinds came to the board and to staff and students, for further workshopping into plans with achievable goals. The unachievable goals remained on the table for inspiration and motivation.

Most of your strategic-planning days won't be like this. Maybe none of them will be. I've only ever had that one experience on anything like that scale. Still, you will sometimes need to take a morning or perhaps a day away from the general work of the board to consider alignment with mission as well as focus on future direction and planning. Having a facilitator assist can result in more efficient work and clearer outcomes.

For these more familiar planning sessions, you can still get input from different stakeholders. There are various ways that can happen. You could canvas stakeholders prior to the planning session. Speak to organisational partners, donors, company members, staff and board directors, about what they perceive to be working well in your ministry as well as what is not working so well. Your facilitator might do this preparatory work for you. Consideration of the responses then becomes part of the agenda for the session. You won't require external input from stakeholders in all your strategy sessions – but you should have it sometimes. It helps guard against insularity.

Having a process as big as the school strategy day requires an extremely skilled facilitator to ensure that it's creatively productive rather than violently chaotic. But if you happen to have one of those highly skilled types nearby – go for it.

23

Will I get paid?

How pleasant it is to have money, heigh ho!

How pleasant it is to have money.

Arthur Hugh Clough, *Dipsychus*

There are no easy answers to this one. 'Possibly, but probably not', is the best I can do.

Traditionally, directorships have not been paid positions in faith-based, not-for-profits. But traditionally, directors have not had to take on the degree of personal risk and responsibility that being a director now requires[1]. Directors have onerous statutory duties and are accountable for their decisions to various stakeholders. They are also at risk of personal liability if they do not exercise their role as director with due diligence.

Sometimes within the one governing organisation (for example, a MPJP[2]) one ministry will pay its board directors while the others do not. Whether or not directors are paid often comes down to the ability of the individual ministry to fund the payment. The unpaid directors are often the ones ministering to the most disenfranchised communities whose ministries struggle to raise the funds necessary to meet essential expenses. It is important to remember that the legal obligations and the risk of liability apply equally to paid and unpaid directors. This is a difficult situation and one that plays out unfairly.

Many board governors (congregations, MPJPs and diocese) are actively looking at this inequity, and some have taken steps to address it. Some ministries have started paying their directors, and in other ministries you might receive an annual honorarium to acknowledge your contribution to your board work.

It's fair to say that not too many directors of faith-based, not-for-profits are in it for the money. We are drawn to this work to live the gospel

message. We partner with sick, young, vulnerable or marginalised people and work with them to create opportunities that will ultimately benefit us all. Our reasons for volunteering haven't changed that much over the years. What has changed is the far more complex and changeable regulatory landscape that we work in.

It's a bit of an easy 'out' to say that because we're not in it for the money, we shouldn't be paid. Payment is not only an acknowledgement of the director's skill, but it can also help increase the extent to which a director is accountable. It's also possible that payment might attract people to the role who would not otherwise be able to consider it, and therefore assist in increasing diversity on our boards.

Payment of board directors is an item on the agenda in many member organisations. I can't guarantee that you will receive payment for your contribution to your ministry (and even if you do get paid, I probably *can* guarantee that it won't represent your true worth!) Still, this is an evolving issue. Watch this space.

24

What if I feel
overwhelmed?

Take from my heart all painful anxiety

Catherine McAuley, *The Suscipe*

The work you are agreeing to take on is significant and impacts people's lives. Most of the time you'll find it deeply satisfying, but sometimes it can also be stressful. Agreeing to take on important work that is sometimes stressful is one thing. Agreeing to take on work that you find is overwhelming you, is another thing altogether. If you are starting to feel overwhelmed, then you need to let the board Chair know. They can only find ways to respond to your stress if they are aware that you are experiencing it.

The Chair is deeply familiar with the organisation, and simply talking through the issues that are weighing upon you might be enough to put your mind at ease. If, for example, you are anxious because you are concerned that you do not really understand the business of the ministry, or perhaps you are confused by the financial reports or you are unclear about the risk management procedures, the Chair can put processes in place to assist you in getting 'up to speed' on those matters. Don't feel embarrassed about talking to the Chair about these concerns. It's part of their role.

It's clearly in everyone's best interests if a discussion about your expectations of the role takes place *before* you have been appointed.[1] It's also part of the role of both the members and the Chair to ensure that new board members have the capacity to manage their role as director, both in terms of skill set and availability. However, if the reality is that those discussions didn't happen when they should have and you now find the amount of work you are doing far exceeds your expectations, you need to address that problem.

- It might be that the workload you are undertaking is in fact in excess of what is expected of you. If so, it's important to clarify that.
- It might be that the workload is only likely to be a short-term issue. Again, the Chair can provide clarity.
- If it is likely to be a long-term issue, you might consider discussing whether or not there is flexibility in the way that the board can make use of your skills. Would it be better for you to be a non-director member of a sub-committee instead? Or can you provide assistance to the board on a more needs-based basis rather than as a board director?

If you are struggling with your relationship with another board member or board members, this is also something the Chair should be able to assist with. Good governance is relational and sometimes intervention by a third party can be very helpful in finding ways to support productive communication. (This might be the Chair themselves or even an external facilitator). This process will include the need for all involved to reflect on their role in the problematic relationship, and to consider strategies for managing conflict more effectively, should it arise again in the future.

If your concern relates to the Chair themselves, then you should still have the conversation with them, in a respectful and understanding way. You are more likely to achieve a good outcome, if you focus on how the Chair's behaviour is impacting upon you, rather than on giving the Chair lots of advice on how they could be a better chair!

Most of the time, the work that you do for your ministry will be engaging, interesting and genuinely satisfying. Most people on ministry boards don't find themselves feeling overwhelmed by their work. In fact, directors often say that they feel energised by it. If you do find yourself experiencing an unreasonable level of stress, it's likely that support will be provided to you by the Chair or other board members, or by the CEO and/or by the company members. If, however, support structures are not provided to you and you continue to feel overwhelmed and unsupported, you have the option of resigning your directorship.

Who runs the place
- the board or
the Executive Director?

I sell here, Sir, what all the world desires to have – POWER.

James Boswell and George Birkbeck Norman Hill, *Life of Johnson* Vol 2

Whenever a new Executive Director takes over from a loved predecessor, it's a bit of an uncertain time for an organisation. It's likely that sooner or later change will be afoot, and not everyone will be happy about it. Who is the author of that change likely to be: the board or the Executive Director?

The answer should be 'both'. The role of the board is to set mission, direction, and policy. The Executive Director works with the board in that process, and then leads implementation of the plan. The appointment of the Executive Director is one of the most important tasks that a board undertakes. They are the face and voice of the organisation, and responsible for the day-to-day running of it. Amongst other things, they oversee the budget and regulatory compliance, manage human resources, oversee marketing and deal with media. They encourage and motivate staff, and in a not-for-profit, possibly volunteers as well. In a faith-based not-for-profit, perhaps their most important task is to embed mission throughout the organisation.

One of the comments you're likely to hear in your travels as a director is 'that's not a matter for the board, that's operational'. It's the Executive Director who runs the ministry, and not the board.

How students are taught in a school is operational. Human resources management is operational. How marketing happens is operational. It's not for the board to tell the marketing manager how to do the marketing. To go back to an earlier example, if a board member is unhappy about the way a particular campaign has been run by the marketing manager (say a campaign has launched that the director believes was poorly designed and is unlikely to reach the target audience), they should not approach the staff member themselves, but raise that concern with the board and the Executive Director.

Similarly, let's say a board director is concerned that a project partner is being treated unfairly by the program manager. That raises a governance concern going to potential breaches of mission and even legislative requirements. The board director should raise their concern with the board and the Executive Director. If the board shares the director's concern, it will ask the Executive Director to investigate and advise.

In a school context, it's not for the school board, for example, to decide what activities should make up the school social justice program. If, however, the school leadership team advise that they plan to disband the social justice program and redistribute that funding toward the music or sports programs, that would be a matter appropriate for the board to raise with the Principal (who is the Executive Director in a school environment).

The Executive Director reports to the board. If the board is concerned about poor performance or inappropriate behaviour on the part of the Executive Director themselves, it's for the board to manage that. In Victoria for example, the Executive Director of a not-for-profit received a great deal of media attention for endorsing a politician during a political campaign. She did so under the banner of the organisation, which was arguably in breach of government rules relating to charities. This raised serious governance issues for that board. If it was found that the law relating to charities had been breached, that would have put the organisation at risk of deregistration, and the negative publicity that followed had the potential to seriously impact donor contributions. For any not-for-profit relying heavily on donor income, reputational risk is one of the most significant risks the organisation faces. The Executive Director was stood down to enable the board to undertake an internal investigation. She eventually resigned.

It is the Executive Director who runs the place, but they do so within the mission and governance framework provided by the board. If the board take the view that the actions of the Executive Director have gone beyond that framework, then it is a matter for the board to determine how serious the offending action is, and how it should be managed.

The Executive Director is appointed and supervised by the board. Ultimately, the buck stops with the board.

26

The board chair –
how hard can it be
to run a meeting?

'Let there be few words and many deeds...'

St Vincent Pallotti

The role of board Chair is onerous. The buck stops with the board, and within the board, the buck stops with the Chair. When people think about the role of the Chair, they are inclined to picture someone sitting at the top end of a long table telling the people around them when they can talk and when they can't. It's important that board meetings are run efficiently and well, but board meetings are probably the least of the Chair's role. At every board meeting, the Chair will have detailed knowledge of all or most of the items on the agenda (which is generally prepared by the CEO and finalised by the Chair a week or so before the meeting). The Chair has gathered that detailed knowledge thanks to all the work they've done since the previous meeting.

Between meetings the Chair might:

- meet with donors who are unhappy about a program closing, and who want reassurance that there were proper grounds for the closure
- meet with donors who are pleased about a new program starting, and who are interested in knowing what more they can do to support it
- meet with other 'like' organisations to discuss sharing resources
- visit new programs to show support for them and to experience the 'on the ground' reality of the work that's being done
- visit existing programs that are not operating effectively
- liaise with company members about the need for new board members
- liaise with sub-committee chairs about compliance requirements
- liaise with sub-committee chairs about the need for new sub-committee members

- attend sub-committee meetings either as a member of that sub-committee or as an ex officio (see glossary) attendee
- read through tenders for a new building project
- meet with the architect and project manager of an ongoing building project
- meet with a neighbouring property owner to discuss the option of leasing additional property
- support board directors who are new, or who require extra support for reasons that might be board-related or personal
- respond quickly to an emerging situation that could result in negative media attention
- write letters and reports
- and much, much, more.

Arguably, more important than all the above is the Chair's relationship with the CEO.

It's a complex relationship. For most board chairs, it is one of the most time-consuming, and hopefully satisfying, aspects of the role. Good governance is relational, and this relationship is one that needs to be particularly high functioning. It's highly collaborative. The Chair and the CEO might occasionally share knowledge about the organisation that is only known to the two of them. The CEO will sometimes use the Chair as a sounding-board for matters that might, for example, include concerns about staff or how to manage a difficult situation with a donor. Similarly, the Chair might offer the CEO informal clarification of the board's general thinking on a particular issue.

But it's a bit of a tricky dance. The board employs the CEO, and it's the board that monitor's the CEO's performance and is ultimately responsible for the decisions made and actions implemented by them. Neither Chair nor CEO must ever lose sight of that responsibility. The Chair should assist the CEO in determining what matters cannot stay just between them but must be put before the board. While the Chair can and should provide advice and support to the CEO, there can be a danger of that support unintentionally leading to 'collusion', where important matters are not put before the board. This raises the risk of 'governance behind closed doors'.

Both the Chair and the CEO must keep the primacy of their respective governance responsibilities at the forefront of their discussions. When in doubt, the default position must always be transparency between the CEO and the board, and not just transparency between the CEO and the board Chair.

It's also very important to remember that the Chair is not the 'other' CEO. The board Chair's role is not to run the operational side of the organisation. That's the role of the CEO. The role of the board, including the board Chair, is to ensure (through all sorts of governance processes) that the CEO does their job well. The CEO is put in an invidious position if the Chair decides to start meddling in and micromanaging operational decisions.

Having said that, in small organisations the reality is that the Chair or other board members will occasionally take on some tasks that are rightly operational. For example, a board member with expertise in communications might sometimes draft a media release for the Executive Director or liaise with the Executive Director on an appropriate response to a media enquiry. The important thing is for all parties to be aware of what boundaries are being crossed and to ensure that it continues only as long as is absolutely necessary.

In some weeks the role of Chair will require daily involvement with the organisation. At other times, two or three weeks might pass with very little input. The amount of work required will vary depending on the organisation. At times, it can be tempting for a board Chair to 'just get the work done' themselves, but a good board Chair ensures that all board members engage in the work of the board (the work of the board – not the work of the organisation), as well as in decision making. An effective board Chair values collaboration.

To be Chair of a faith based not-for-profit requires time, dedication to mission, and ability. It's also likely to be challenging, frustrating, unpaid (or poorly paid) and enormously satisfying.

27

Will I have to
'lean in'?

I must have my share in the conversation.

Jane Austen, *Pride and Prejudice*

In 2013, Sheryl Sandberg, who was then Chief Operating Officer of Facebook, published *Lean in: Women, work and the will to lead.* The book went on to become a bestseller, and the phrase 'Lean in' became a cultural phenomenon. Sandberg's argument was that women can 'have it all' (or at least have more than they're used to), if they stand up and demand it within their workplaces. This became something of a catchcry: that in striving for equal pay, promotion prospects and work conditions, women, like men, should 'lean in' and make their voices heard by the people that matter.

I first heard the phrase 'lean in' from a school principal. She told me that the school her daughter attended (not her own) was implementing a 'lean in' program for their female students. The impetus for the new program was at least partly due to numerous studies that show that in conversations involving both men and women, men dominate the conversation space. The aim of this program was, amongst other things, to teach the young women to 'lean in' and express their own opinions and thoughts with the same confidence as the men around them.

My reaction to hearing about the program was mixed. I could certainly see benefit in tackling head-on the traditional cultural restraints preventing young women from speaking up for themselves, particularly in formal situations such as meetings or seminars. However, as someone who had spent a lot of time in meetings, I was also a little bit horrified. In my experience, the problem isn't that women don't say enough – it's that some people (often but not always men) take up more than their share of board oxygen, by saying too much. Rather than telling women it's always their responsibility to 'lean in', why not build in a little bit of 'lean out' for the over-sharers instead?

Board members can feel pressured to contribute to a discussion for the sake of contributing. This is understandable, particularly when the board member is new to the board and may feel that they need to justify their inclusion in the group. Sitting back, and taking time to listen, absorb and question is prudent and smart. It won't be held against you. Asking questions is often particularly useful for helping new members find their way.

It would be an interesting exercise over the course of a meeting for board members to ask themselves, what does my comment or question add to the board discussion? I know that might sound harsh. I'm certainly not advocating introducing a 'relevance scale' to determine whether a comment should be made, or a question asked. Not every comment needs to be deeply insightful, and sometimes the 'this is a really dumb question' questions, are really good ones. I'm also not arguing in favour of soulless, intense meetings. There are definitely times for a funny comment or an interesting aside, because these things *do* add to the discussion, perhaps to ease a tense moment or add to a sense of camaraderie within the group.

The time-wasting, oxygen-sucking contributions that I'm talking about are the ones that seem to pop into a board member's head and straight onto the board table, without filter. We have all had the experience – whether in work meetings, school information nights, political events, or even at dinner parties – of people who need to speak, solely for the sake of speaking and for no other purpose. I have sat in meetings that have gone much longer than they should because people unnecessarily take up time:

- repeating what's already been said, often word for word, or
- saying something that leaves everyone else shaking their heads in confusion because it clearly doesn't have anything to do with the discussion at hand, or
- laboriously explaining the blindingly obvious (yes, 'mansplaining').

So, leaving behind the unfiltered, wordy time bombs, women, by all means 'lean in'! The same goes for men and people of *all* genders, binary and non-binary. Please contribute your thoughts and questions in meetings with confidence. You won't go wrong, provided you do so with respect for all around you and with an understanding that you don't need to impress anyone on the board. The fact that you have been invited to become a director is evidence that you have skill or wisdom or experience that is useful to the board. No-one needs to prove that they're a star. From here on, it's a team effort.

What on earth is an MPJP?

'That sounds like nonsense my dear.'

'May be so, my dear; but it may be very good law for all that.'

Sir Walter Scott, *Guy Mannering*

What happens to sisters, priests, and brothers as they age? As congregations become smaller, who ensures that the last remaining members are cared for physically, mentally, and spiritually? What happens to congregational assets? And perhaps most importantly for the congregational members themselves, what legacy of their life's work lives on?

The legacy question is central to the momentum for incorporation of church ministries. The transfer of power from religious congregations to company boards is a practical response to the reality of aging populations. Trustees and directors who are stepping into the shoes of the last of the active members of religious orders should be mindful of the enormity of the change taking place in the transfer of governance, and the profundity of the impact of that change, both on individual sisters, priests, and brothers, and on the congregations of religious as a whole.

You might sometimes hear Ministerial Public Juridic Persons, or MPJPs, referred to as PJPs. PJPs (Public Juridic Persons) have been around a bit longer. Dioceses, parishes and religious congregations are all PJPs. MPJPs are a relatively new form of entity in the Catholic Church. MPJPs have both canonical and civil authority. They are an important response to the legacy question. As many religious congregations face the reality that they are likely to come to an end in the foreseeable future due to aging membership, they have needed to find a way to ensure that their work and mission continue beyond their own existence. What happens to all the schools and hospitals that are owned by religious congregations, when those congregations no longer exist? The church has responded to this need by enabling the creation of MPJPs.

MPJPs are legal entities into which ministries can be transferred. Governance of those ministries then transfers to the trustees of the MPJP. The trustees might be a mix of religious and lay people or they are often only lay people. Each MPJP is a legal entity in its own right and has its own governance structure. Approval for the creation of an MPJP needs to be obtained from the Vatican or a local bishop.

The board directors of an MPJP (who are often referred to as either 'trustees' or 'trustee directors') effectively step into the shoes of the previous congregational owners. They take over ownership of land and property relating to the ministries that are transferred into the MPJP. The MPJP structure should support good governance by improving transparency and accountability in faith-based ministries, as well as by enabling far greater diversity of leadership. The various ministries that previously reported to the religious congregation now report to the MPJP Trustees. The Trustees of an MPJP must conform to two distinct legal codes: canonical (church) law and civil law (e.g. corporations law). Having the rights and responsibilities that comes with this combined authority, enables them to continue to govern these ministries long after the religious congregation that established them has ceased to exist.

As MPJPs have stepped into the role of the previous congregational or diocesan owner, they also have the authority to make formal comment on behalf of the church. It will be interesting to what extent this opportunity is taken up by the various MPJPs as they become more established.

An MPJP might consist of the ministries of one religious order only, or the ministries of several orders. For example, Mercy Partners (based in Queensland) is responsible for ministries that previously belonged to the Queensland Sisters of the Presentation of the Blessed Virgin Mary (Presentations), Queensland and Parramatta Sisters of Mercy (Mercys) and the Missionary Franciscan Sisters of the Immaculate Conception (Franciscans) Orders. Kildare Ministries (based in Victoria) governs ministries that were previously owned by the Brigidine Sisters of New South Wales and Victoria and The Victorian Presentation Sisters. You might have noted (to confuse matters), that a single Order of sisters, brothers or priests might have different congregations in different MPJPs.

Let's say your community service ministry was originally created by the Brigidine sisters. It was incorporated by the sisters some years ago, so it now has a board of directors (which you are about to join) who are responsible for governance of that company. The members or owners of the company at the time of incorporation were the Brigidine sisters and so, at that time, the board reported to those sisters. Subsequently, the sisters created Kildare Ministries, and transferred all their Brigidine ministries into that MPJP. The MPJP takes over legal responsibility for all the ministries now in it and, rather than reporting to the Brigidine sisters, your board now reports to Kildare Ministries.

What happens if the members (or owners) disagree with the Board's decision?

We none of us expect to be in smooth water all our days.

Jane Austen, *Persuasion*.

In most cases, the short answer to this question is 'nothing'. The board derives its decision-making authority from the company's constitution, which specifies the roles and responsibilities of the board and the members and sets out rules about meetings. In church based not-for-profits, the reason for the establishment of an independent incorporated board is often to enable the members to divest themselves of the everyday governance responsibilities of their ministries. For that reason, the authority to make nearly all decisions relating to governance of the ministry vests in the board and not with the members.

A slightly longer answer to the question elicits a slightly more complicated response.

Company members retain 'big-picture' governance responsibility for their ministries. They do not attend board meetings and do not have voting power when it comes to board decisions. They know what decisions are made by the board because they receive the minutes of board meetings. There is frequently some lag time, however, between the meeting and the minutes being provided to the members. Traditionally, minutes are drafted after a board meeting and circulated to the board directors. The board directors can then suggest changes, if they do not believe the draft is an accurate representation of the meeting. It is only after the minutes are formally ratified as being an accurate record of the meeting and signed by the board Chair, that they can be forwarded to the company members in their final, approved form. That approval often doesn't take place until the following board meeting, often a month or more later.

If the company members are unhappy with a decision of the board, they do not normally have the power to take direct action. However, it's not entirely accurate to say that they can do nothing. Under the constitution, members retain 'reserve powers' which, as the name implies, are powers not granted to the company but retained by the members. While reserve powers are usually quite limited in number, they are significant powers. They are likely to include:

- purchase/sale of property
- limits on financial transactions (such as bank loans) above a set amount
- changes to mission/vision
- *and* the power to both appoint and remove directors.

While the power of appointment and removal is a potentially a potent weapon, it is a very blunt one for the members to attempt to use over a single decision. Decisions are made by the board and not by individual directors, and the reputational risk to the ministry of the members taking action against the whole or part of the board would be significant. They would be unlikely to do so. Circumstances where they might choose to act could include a gross breach of mission and/or fiduciary duty on the part of a director or directors.

Of course, it's also possible for board directors to disagree with the decisions of the members. At times, I have been very frustrated by the decisions made by members not to accept the recommendations made by our board for appointment of new directors. Members often reserve the power of appointment of new directors, but the (often time-consuming) work of finding them is frequently left to the board.

The two best ways to avoid destructive dysfunction between the members and the Board are:

- to ensure that the mission of the ministry remains aligned with the mission of the members, and
- ongoing, effective communication.

It's incumbent on the members to ensure that the directors they appoint understand and support the mission of the ministry. Overseeing alignment with mission is perhaps the members' most important role. It's also important that directors are appointed because they have skills that will be valuable to the ministry, and not just because they are 'good people' (although, there may occasionally be times when that is exactly the skill that a board is looking for).

Of course it is also an essential part of governance for the board to ensure that the mission and vision of the ministry remains aligned with that of the members. In a well-governed, well-functioning ministry, communication between the members and the board (particularly the board Chair) will be transparent and regular. Most ministries will have an Annual General Meeting each year, which is the formal process for the ministry to report to the members on the previous year's performance. Ideally, however, there will also be a number of more informal opportunities for connection during the year. Good governance is relational, and maintaining regular communication assists in all parties to remain united in outlook, even if not always in agreement on every detail.

We've done 'mission', so can we start work now?

Change your opinions, keep to your principles;
change your leaves, keep intact your roots.

Victor Hugo, *Intellectual Autobiography*

Your board has done all the hard work of coming up with excellent mission, vision and values statements. So, does that mean you're off the hook? Is it all over for mission and time to get on with the 'real' work?

Well, no.

Let's say that outreach is a central part of your mission. What does that mean? How do you comply with that mission? Does 'reaching out' mean wandering the nearby streets in search of people in need? That's exactly the mission that many faith-based ministries existing today were founded on. Today, literally wandering through the streets is probably neither the most practical nor effective outreach option for most ministries (although it remains at the heart of some). So how *do* you go about finding the families, individuals, or groups in need in your community? How do they find you? Does your 'outreach' actually reach outward, or do you find yourself only helping those families who come onto your ministry radar because they're referred to you by a closed referral system (by other families, staff, or historical reasons, etc.)? It's fine to have an active system of internal referrals, but is that the best way to fulfil your mission?

Questions about mission can get very messy, very quickly. Does charity begin at home? Let's work through a school example:

- Does your school, whose mission statement specifically refers to supporting 'at risk' students, offer financial support to your existing student whose family is asset-rich but is going through an income poor phase?
    - This doesn't sound like it directly fits your mission, but it would probably be reasonable to provide the support for a limited period of time – probably with an expectation that the fees will be repaid, at least in part, in due course.

- What about the Year 10 student whose parents have just been killed in a car accident?
  - That obviously fits the mission.
- What if instead of being in Year 10, that student is about to start Year 7, and will require a full scholarship for the entirety of her time at the school?
  - That will be a significant and ongoing financial contribution for the school to make, but surely it fits the mission requirements.
- Will you also take on her 2 younger siblings, who are still in primary school?
- What about their primary school 'step siblings': the 2 children belonging to the foster family who have opened their home to take on these three extra children, and who are themselves taking a significant financial hit as a result?
- In the meantime, what about the two children of a homeless dad who's just applied for support?
- What impact on your bottom line would agreeing to support all these students have?
  - While you have a mission to support at-risk students, you also have a legal obligation to keep the ministry financially viable.
- What about the families who are not in desperate circumstances, but who cannot afford to send their child(ren) to your school unless they get financial assistance?
- Does it matter whether the family shares the school's faith tradition? Should it matter?
- Part of a faith-based school's mission is likely to be to provide a rich experience of liturgy, prayer, and spirituality. How does that weigh against the other needs?

Having sat on a needs-based scholarship committee of a Catholic girl's secondary college, I can say that these are realistic scenarios. Mission-based decisions crop up for our ministries in all sorts of ways. Should you accept funding from gambling organisations? Should you sell that property for less than market value, to ensure it will be developed in a way that is environmentally sustainable and community friendly? (Which would be in accordance with the *Laudato Si'* Action Platform.[1]) For years now church-based schools have been quietly accepting and supportive of gender and sexually diverse students – putting practical measures in place such as gender non-specific toilets and making school uniform changes to better meet the needs of the whole student group. This issue has been a complex one for Catholic schools, in light of church teaching on sexuality and gender.

In their recently released advice: Created and Loved, a Guide for Catholic Schools on Identity and Gender[2], the Australian Catholic Bishops Conference has provided greater clarity around these issues. The bishops have affirmed that providing unisex toilets and changerooms, together with flexibility in uniform requirements, supports access and safety for potentially vulnerable students and caters to 'the diversity of the student body'.

When your ministry is faced with uncertainty and difficult decision-making, it's having your mission, vision and values embedded throughout the organisation that guides you. From them come the clear governance processes you require, including meaningful policies and procedures, good risk-management processes and regular mission formation at board level. These governance processes help to ensure that your decisions are transparent and accountable to the whole of the ministry body. We can't solve every social, education, health, disability, aged care, justice or inequity problem that our ministries are designed to address, and we

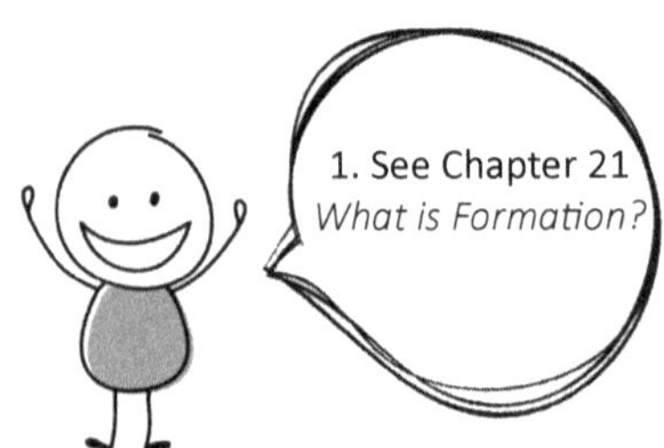

can't help every person in need of assistance. Messy, difficult decisions will always need to be made. When making them, we need clear, mission-based criteria to apply to our decision-making, and we need to make sure that the criteria remain relevant, active and ongoing.

Because mission is a verb.

2. Created and Loved, a guide for Catholic schools on identity and gender, Australian Catholic Bishops Conference, https://bit.ly/CreatedandLoved

31

Did someone
mention
a pilgrimage?

Redy to wenden on my pilgrimage

To Caunterbury with ful devout corage…

Geoffrey Chaucer, *The Canterbury Tales.*

If you are very fortunate indeed, part of the formation you receive into the faith tradition and culture of your ministry might include having the opportunity to go on pilgrimage. Some faith-based ministries provide this opportunity to select members of the ministry including staff, executive management and board directors.

A pilgrimage is a journey to a sacred place. It's difficult to explain the extent to which the physical act of travel impacts upon this ancient form of spiritual seeking. It's a faith experience, but you don't need to share the faith tradition of your ministry for a pilgrimage to be both profound and moving.

Pilgrimages vary, but within ministry not-for-profits they generally involve travelling to the home of the individual who established the religious order or faith ministry, in whose mission and tradition your organisation was created. I have been fortunate to have experienced two pilgrimages. Both were to Ireland, and both were in honour of women who were extraordinary, although I suspect that neither of them would have described themselves in that way.

Catherine McAuley founded the Sisters of Mercy, in Dublin in 1831. My pilgrimage to Dublin was shared with other people working in Mercy Ministries. They included teachers, health workers, an archivist, eco-spirituality workers, and several board director volunteers. We spent a week gathered in the beautiful, large Baggot Street house that Catherine built (almost literally, as she was the project manager). She built the house with her private funds to support women and children in need in the 1800s Ireland. We travelled to her early home and walked the same streets of Dublin that she had walked. We heard about her life, and her struggles with the church hierarchy. We heard about the women and children she supported, and about the depth of her compassion, warmth, and hospitality. We also learned about the ways in which her influence continues in the large number of ministries worldwide that still come under the auspices of the Sisters of Mercy, internationally.

While I did not attend a formal pilgrimage for Nano Nagle, who was the founder of the Presentation of the Blessed Virgin Mary sisters (the Presentations), I was fortunate enough to be supported by the Presentation Sisters in undertaking my own Nano Nagle pilgrimage while I was in Ireland. In Cork, I was taken on a tour around the streets and laneways where Nano once wandered with her lamp, searching out women in need. I stayed in Ballygriffin, Nano's birthplace, and home to a heritage centre in her honour. It's a beautiful, tranquil spot, nestled in the heart of the Blackwater Valley.

These experiences change you in unexpected ways. I all but saw both women stand and shake off the musty historical pages that had bound them. The holy, conservative nuns who had lived in my previous consciousness evaporated into fierce advocates for underprivileged women. At times they were each prevented by church leaders from achieving what they wanted to achieve, and they struggled to deal with their anger and frustration. Both relied on their faith to continue their work for marginalised women in their communities, despite the sometimes-bitter disappointments they endured. They created new paths and new opportunities for themselves; for the women who came to work with them, and for the many women they supported.

A great pilgrimage lights a fire in your belly. It leads you to see, in a very practical way, that the work we do in our ministries doesn't happen in a vacuum. It is part of a large, historical and ongoing story of faith-filled commitment to supporting marginalised people.

Not all board directors will have the opportunity to go on pilgrimage. If you are one of those lucky enough to have that opportunity present itself to you, my advice is to grab it with both hands, and run.

32

Why does
board history
matter?

The best prophet of the future is the past.

Lord Byron, *Journal* 1821

When I was a newly minted director of a faith-based not-for-profit who undertook international development work, I was part of a decision-making process to withdraw financial support from a country where we no longer had 'in country' oversight. An education program had run there for several years, administered by many sisters over time. The last of those sisters had returned to Australia for health reasons, and she had no obvious successor. The decision for us as a board was straightforward. There was no-one to run the program, and it was not a program model that had the potential to become self-sustaining, which had become one of our program criteria. At the time, we were in receipt of applications for financial support from other regions closer to Australia where we had staff 'in country', and where the programs aligned more clearly with our development criteria. The decision to end the program was the obvious choice to make, and it was the right choice. The company members were aware of our decision and agreed with it.

What we did not do, however, was consider carefully enough (or at all) the effect of that decision on the many sisters who had worked in that program, and who remained emotionally tied to it. That would not have changed our decision, but it would have changed our response to it. We should have sought out those sisters who we knew would be affected by it and sought an opportunity to meet with them. They may or may not have understood or approved of our decision, but at least we would have shown respect for their years of commitment to the people they worked with and for. Instead, they heard about the decision on the grapevine along with everyone else, and they were shocked, hurt, and angry. I discovered just how hurt and angry at a conference that I attended with several of them. I arrived at this conference not knowing either them or their history. It didn't take long for the depth of their anger to be made clear to me. I didn't know the history of the program and hadn't thought to ask. Our board had stepped into the shoes of these women and walked off along an entirely new path as though they'd never existed.

It's important to understand the history of your ministry. It helps to inform your decisions, even when the decisions you make today are very different from the decisions that would have been made in time gone by. A small group of us offering to meet with the sisters who were impacted by our decision would not have changed the bottom line. It would, however, have allowed us to listen to the stories of their time overseas and to consider whether there might be a way that we could honour their commitment there, as it had been such a significant commitment.

Good governance is relational.

33

Did Someone
Say Synodality?

Let us not soundproof our hearts; let us not remain barricaded in our certainties.

Pope Francis. *Homily*, Mass for opening of the Synodal Path

In the Catholic lexicon, 'synodality' means 'walking together'. Synods have been part of the governance process of the church since ancient times. Traditionally, synods have been clerical affairs, and the walking has been done by bishops alone. Pope Francis, however, has expressed his support for the collaborative possibilities of synodality and, in October 2021, commenced a two-year process for the Catholic Church to have a 'synod on synodality'. Unlike previous synods, this one is not entirely limited to bishops. The purpose of the synod is for the Church to consider ways in which it can become more 'synodal' or inclusive in its governance processes. Francis has called for openness, collaboration and mutual listening within this process – of working out a process.

I can't help but wonder why, in embracing a process that is in some ways radical for the church, in that it calls for the inclusion of lay people in the discussion, they have chosen a word which is so obscure and non-inclusive. 'Synodality' has a flavour of exclusion because who knows what it means? For those who do know what it means, it's associated with the 'Curia Club'. However, as Francis' call is at least a step in the right governance direction, we probably need to take deep breaths and absorb the obscure name.

Whether the process will have any significant impact on issues confronting the church such as the role of women in the church, the involvement of lay people in church governance and the need for diversity in church leadership, remains to be seen.

What I do know is that all these things are *already* being lived by the board directors of church-based, not-for-profit ministries. Lots of board directors and board Chairs are women. Our work is highly collaborative, and if our boards have excellent governance processes, they are open and transparent, and encouraging of mutual listening. Not all of our boards are as diverse as they could or should be – but they are working towards that goal. I recently heard the former President of Ireland, Mary

McAleese speaking on synodality (she didn't like the word either). She commented on the fact that it's the everyday people of God who are out there doing the work of the church, and they're doing it without fanfare, and often without financial reward, in thousands of church-based, not-for-profit ministries.

Blessings to you all for that (synodal) generosity of heart, skill and spirit.

34

What's in
it for me?

When I'm not thanked at all, I'm thanked enough,

I've done my duty, and I've done no more.

Henry Fielding, *Tom Thumb the Great.*

After I had my first baby, I left private legal practice to work part-time at a Community Legal Centre in Broadmeadows – a suburb of Melbourne that has a vibrant, ethnically diverse community, but which also faces significant challenges. Many of the families I worked with struggled to find affordable housing. Meeting living costs was a constant challenge. Whatever Instagram might tell us, 'wealth' means having secure housing and the means to buy food and medication, without forgoing necessities such as washing powder and shampoo.

I had previously volunteered at two other Community Legal Centres, so I thought I had a pretty good understanding of what I was letting myself in for. I was keen to start this new job because I wanted 'to help'. Fortunately for everyone, I got over that.

My legal service clients and the community of partners that we work with in our not-for-profit ministries, share something in common. They often come from marginalised communities, and as community members or as individuals, they often have little or no voice. What they need more than help, is respect. Of course, our aim *is* to help these communities, but we do that as their partners and colleagues, and not as their 'helpers'. We strive with them toward equality of opportunity, so that they no longer need to rely on our 'help'.

For a while, in that first role, I had the balance wrong. I genuinely wanted to help, and I was a little offended when I didn't get (what I considered to be) appropriate appreciation for my good efforts. I'd left a well-paid job, and the Legal Service was lucky to have me! I was stuck in the hierarchy, and although I certainly couldn't admit it to myself at the time, part of me was looking forward to soaking up the martyr glory of undertaking good works. My clients were juggling far too many complex needs to indulge me.

So, what's *not* in it for you when it comes to joining the board of a church-based ministry, is martyr glory. What you *do* get is much deeper.

- Of course, you'll make friends. They might be friends that you end up catching up with regularly, or friends who you only see through your ministry work, but you'll get to know people with different backgrounds, interests, and stories. You'll come to know them well, because you'll be engaging with them on issues such as the meaning and effect of marginalisation, as well as the impact of interest rate changes, as well as the need for new board members, as well as some recipe swapping (that last one may not be for everyone, but it's certainly been my experience).
- There will be times when you'll feel overwhelmed by seeing what your ministry has been able to achieve. You'll watch students advocate for climate change measures. You'll listen to refugees speak of the life-changing effect that your mentoring program has had on the lives of them and their families and hear about how they are now themselves mentors in that same program. You'll sit with First Nations people and learn about the impact that your potential health program could have on the well-being of their community. You'll hear from volunteers about the impact on the elderly and isolated partners with whom they work, of their regular, ongoing relationship.
- You'll be frustrated by:
  - lack of funds
  - other board members
  - staff not pulling their weight
  - lack of political interest in your mission.
- You'll be deeply moved by:
  - generosity from unexpected quarters
  - other board members
  - staff going above and beyond the call of duty
  - your ability to impact change.

Christ was drawn to the marginalised, and they to him. He reached out to women (deeply marginalised in his society), the poor, the sick and the excluded. He was a marginalised figure himself. While mission varies from ministry to ministry, it all comes back in some form to Christ's call for us to heed and respond to the needs of the vulnerable and excluded, by walking alongside them. When we do so, we are not doing it just for them, but also for ourselves, and in fact, for us all.

Reflections and prayers

(A good way to start a meeting of a board or a committee with a mission of governance.)

1. (Religious)

Let us take a moment to acknowledge the traditional custodians of the land on which we are gathered today, the (name your local Indigenous people or peoples). We pay respect to their elders past present and future. We ask that we might take care of the mission entrusted to us with the same wisdom as our Indigenous people cared for their land for so many generations.

Let us take a few moments as we come together, just to be quiet to bring our focus into this place, to put aside all the other concerns in our life, to be at peace with each other.

(Long pause)

Loving God, we thank you for your trust in us.

You know that we are ordinary people.

But you have great hopes for us and for the work we are guiding and supporting.

Help us to listen to each other, to speak constructively and to respect our colleagues.

You call us to share a vision and work as one.

We pray for those in our ministry who may need special prayers at this time (we can recall the sick, the bereaved and also those blessed in some special way).

We call on the guidance of you Holy Spirit in these ancient words:

Come Holy Spirit, fill the hearts of your faithful, enkindle in them the fire of your love. Send forth your spirit Lord, and they will be created and you will renew the face of the earth. Amen.

– Michael McGirr

2. (Not religious)

We take a moment to acknowledge the traditional custodians of the land on which we are gathered today, the (name your local Indigenous people or peoples). We pay respect to their elders past, present and future.

Let us pause a moment before we get down to business.

Take a moment to look at who else is in the meeting with us.

Maybe we know some of our colleagues well, maybe some not so well.

Let's take a moment to remember that each person brings a world of experience with them to this gathering.

Some are having a good day, some not so good.

Some have worries at home, some are excited by life.

We are all human. We all share a journey.

For the next little while our paths come together.

Let us treat each other with respect and consideration,

Let us try to listen and learn from each other,

To treat each other as a blessing, not part of a machine.

However mundane this meeting,

Let us hope that our work adds something to the well-being of the human family

And helps build a more just world.

Each item on the agenda has somebody's well-being attached to it.

Let us be present to this group,

Because all life is a gift and a mystery.

Let us honour the source of that life and that gift

By our kindness and openness.

– Michael McGirr

3. (Religious)

We take a moment to acknowledge the traditional custodians of the land on which we are gathered today, the (name your local Indigenous people or peoples). We pay respect to their elders past, present and future. We ask for healing and reconciliation between all God's people.

Loving God,

Your son Jesus helps us to understand that everyone belongs to your family.

He met so many different people: women and men, young and old, powerful and powerless.

He had a heart for them all, especially those of least account.

May we bring the same heart to this gathering.

May we be open to all people and honest in our attempts to help others.

May we find your presence in our responsibilities, in the question asked of us, in the challenges we face.

Sometimes we are daunted by our task

But we trust in you to support us and guide us.

Today we remember (chance to pray for colleagues, staff etc)

Jesus said 'come to me'. He also said 'go out to the world.'

May all our comings and goings be part of a journey in faith

As we work to build the kingdom which Jesus compared to a pearl of great price.

We ask this in your name. Amen.

– Michael McGirr

4. (More traditional religious)

We take a moment to acknowledge the traditional custodians of the land on which we are gathered today, the (name your local Indigenous people or peoples). We pay respect to their elders past, present and future.

Let us begin our meeting with the wonderful prayer of St Francis.

Lord, make me an instrument of your peace:
where there is hatred, let me sow love;
where there is injury, pardon;
where there is doubt, faith;
where there is despair, hope;
where there is darkness, light;
where there is sadness, joy.

O divine Master, grant that I may not so much seek
to be consoled as to console,
to be understood as to understand,
to be loved as to love.
For it is in giving that we receive,
it is in pardoning that we are pardoned,
and it is in dying that we are born to eternal life.
Amen.

– Michael McGirr

5. (Non-religious)

We take a moment to acknowledge the traditional custodians of the land on which we are gathered today, the (name your local Indigenous people or peoples). We pay respect to their elders past, present and future.

Let us be still and try to centre ourselves.

Let us try to be present to each other and present in this space.

Before we set out on our meeting,

Perhaps we can look back over the last day or so.

Did anything special happen that we were too busy or preoccupied to notice?

Did we have any worries or frustrations or annoyances we might still be carrying?

What made us laugh?

What filled us with hope? (a pause here)

We bring our whole selves to every meeting.

Thinking over one day reminds us how many people and events make us who we are.

Every day is shaping us.

So let's begin our meeting on a note of gratitude for the wonder of life

In all its glorious complexity

And all its delightful simplicity.

Peace!

– Michael McGirr

Glossary

Canon law

- A set of rules and legal principles (known as the 'Code of Canon Law') made and enforced by church authority, that sets out regulatory requirements for Catholic church organisations.

Compliance

- Compliance in a governance context refers to regulatory compliance. An organisation must comply with the laws, regulations, policies and procedures that apply to it. Compliance involves not only meeting those requirements but reporting to the relevant authority to confirm they have been met.

Congregation (Religious Congregation)

- There are historical and canonical distinctions between Religious Orders and Religious Congregations, which relate to whether the vows taken upon entering were 'solemn' (to enter an Order) or 'simple' (to join a Congregation). The distinction originally related to whether the religious group was enclosed. Members of Religious Congregations are referred to as 'Religious'. More recently, the distinction between the two has been somewhat blurred. In the context of this text, a Congregation refers to a Religious Congregation of sisters, priests or brothers.

Constitution (company)

- The constitution sets out the rights and responsibilities of the members and directors of the company. It also sets out rules, such as those governing the requirements for board meetings.

Director

- Someone appointed as a director of a company in accordance with the constitution of that company.

Executive Director (CEO or Principal)

- The leader of the operational arm of the organisation. The Executive Director is sometimes called the Chief Executive Officer or CEO. In church-based schools governed by incorporated boards, the Executive Director is the school Principal.

Ex officio

- A person who holds a board role because of their position, rather than in their personal capacity. For example, a board Chair might be an *ex officio* member of a board subcommittee. If the Chair finishes in their role as Chair, their role on the subcommittee will also cease and be transferred to the new Chair.

Fiduciary Duty

- A fiduciary duty is a duty to act with care, diligence and undivided loyalty toward the ministry or organisation of which you are a director, over and above any other interest, including personal interest.

For purpose organisation

- An organisation with a socially/environmentally progressive mission which is embedded across its business structures and processes, but which operates on a 'for profit' basis. Some traditionally not-for-profit organisations are now rebranding as 'for purpose', on the basis that no organisation can continue to operate without profit.

Formation

- Formation is the process of being 'formed' in the tradition and culture of the organisation that you are joining. It's a form of spiritual and educational training.

Foundational documents

- These documents are the company mission statement, vision statement and values.

In camera

- This literally means 'in private'. You are likely to have an *in camera* session at the end of each board meeting (or at the end of some meetings) with board members only, and without any members of staff, including the Executive Director. The board should also have an annual *in camera* meeting with the external auditors.

Governance

- Governance is a process to ensure the effective and efficient running of an organisation. It encompasses rules, policies, procedures, practice, and culture, designed to provide transparency, accountability, integrity and successful operation.

Limited liability

- A director of a company limited by guarantee is not personally liable for the debts incurred by the company, except in exceptional circumstances (such as if they breach their fiduciary duty to the company).

MPJP (or Ministerial Public Juridic Person)

- MPJPs are a legal entity within the Catholic church. They are created by approval of either the Vatican or bishops and have both civil and canonical (or church) authority. A number of religious congregations have taken steps to transfer governance of their ministries into MPJP's.

Member

- The member is the owner of the company. In a faith-based not for profit organisation, it is likely to be a religious congregation or a ministerial public juridic person (MPJP) or a diocese or archdiocese.

Ministry

- 'Company', 'organisation' and 'ministry' are largely interchangeable labels in faith-based organisations. 'Ministry' is, however, more reflective of a mission of outreach than 'company'.

Minutes

- Minutes are a written record of decision making and relevant discussion at board meetings. They are not and should not be a transcript of the meeting. The minutes of each meeting must be approved by the board as being an accurate record of the meeting. Minutes might be taken by the company secretary, or the board might have a minute taker who is independent of the board. The Chair would usually check the draft minutes before circulation to Board members.

Mission

- Mission is the heart of what your organisation exists to do. It's why you're there. Your mission should be *the* motivation for everyone engaged in your ministry (board, staff, volunteers). What that mission is, will vary from organisation to organisation.

Mission statement

- Creating a mission statement is part of the strategic role of the board. The statement is a concise summation of the purpose or mission of the organisation. The mission statement should be embedded throughout the organisation.

Not-for-profit

- As the name implies, not-for-profit organisations operate for the benefit of the community rather than to create profit for the owners or anyone else.

Orders (or Religious Orders)

- There are historical and canonical distinctions between Religious Orders and Religious Congregations, which relate to whether the vows taken upon entering were 'solemn' (to enter an Order) or 'simple' (to join a Congregation). The distinction originally concerned whether or not the religious group was enclosed. More recently, the distinction between the two has been somewhat blurred.

Outreach

- Outreach is the provision of support to communities in need, by working with those communities to determine the type of support required.

National Redress Scheme

- This scheme was established following the findings of the Royal Commission into Institutional Responses to Child Sexual Abuse. The scheme was implemented by the Commonwealth Government to provide compensation and other support including counselling, for victims of institutionalised sexual abuse. The Catholic Church has joined the scheme.

Reserve powers

- In the company constitution, members may retain specific powers, rather than granting them to the board. These powers are therefore 'reserved' by the members and are known as reserve powers. Reserve Powers in church based not-for-profits most commonly relate to the power to appoint and dismiss directors.

Risk management

- Risk management is the process of identifying, assessing, prioritizing and managing the various risks that apply to an organisation. Risk can be financial, reputational, physical or more. It is not about eradicating risk, but having systems in place to manage it appropriately.

Royal Commission into Institutional Responses to Child Sexual Abuse

- The Commission was established by the Commonwealth government in January 2013 to investigate the sexual abuse of children (and the cover-up of that abuse) in various religious, sporting and other institutions, including the Catholic Church. Its findings were made public in December 2017.

Safeguarding

- Safeguarding is the process put in place by an organisation to protect from harm (particularly physical harm or sexual abuse), the people with whom they interact. The term is most often used in relation to the protection of children and adults at risk

Strategic direction

- This is the plan put in place by an organisation to meet its short, medium and long-term goals.

Values statement

- Your values statement defines the values under which your organisation operates. Your mission statement sets out what it is that your organisation is there to do, and the values statement guides the decision making necessary to meet the organisations goals.

Vision statement

- This is aspirational. It sets out your future objectives. It must align with your mission and values, and in faith-based not-for-profits, it should also make reference to how your vision will impact your community and the community or communities with whom you are working.

Epigraph Bibliography

What, exactly, is a board? ....p 13

In the beginning...

Genesis 1:1, NRSV Bible

What sort of people become board directors? ....p 19

Great actions speak great minds, and such should govern...

Beaumont F and Fletcher J, The Prophetess, Project Gutenberg, https://www.gutenberg.org/files/45780/45780-h/45780-h.htm, accessed 20 December 2022.

What is governance anyway? ....p 23

...all things should be done decently and in order.

1 Corinthians 14:4, NRSV Bible

Why does governance matter? ....p 27

You shall not, for the sake of one individual, change the meaning of principle and integrity.

Austen J, Pride and prejudice (1813), Project Gutenberg, https://www.gutenberg.org/files/1342/1342-h/1342-h.htm, accessed 20 December 2022.

Do I have to behave like a 'nun'? ....p 31

My idea of good company, Mr Elliot, is the company of clever, well-informed people, who have a great deal of conversation.

Austen J, Persuasion (1817), Project Gutenberg, https://www.gutenberg.org/files/105/105-h/105-h.htm, accessed 20 December 2022.

Why all the fuss about 'mission'? ....p 35

What do we live for, if it is not to make life less difficult to each other?

Eliot G (Mary Anne Evans), Middlemarch (1871), Project Gutenberg, https://www.gutenberg.org/files/145/145-h/145-h.htm, accessed 20 December 2022.

Is mission more important than governance? .... p 39

If you have built castles in the air, your work need not be lost; that is where they should be. Now put the foundations under them.

Thoreau HD, Waldon (1854), Project Gutenberg, https://www.gutenberg.org/files/205/205-h/205-h.htm, accessed 20 December 2022.

What questions should I ask before starting? .... p 43

The man who asks a question is a fool for a minute, the man who does not ask is a fool for life

Widely attributed online to Confucius, despite there being no evidence of his ever having said it.

Will everyone be older/younger /smarter than me? .... p 47

And, above all things, never think that you're not good enough yourself. (...) My belief is that in life people will take you very much at your own reckoning.

Trollope A, The Small House at Allington (1864), Project Gutenberg, https://www.gutenberg.org/files/4599/4599-h/4599-h.htm, accessed 20 December 2022.

Are there risks involved in joining a board? .... p 51

My only solution for the problem of habitual accidents...is for everyone to stay in bed all day. Even then, there is always the chance that you will fall out.

Benchley R, Chips off the Old Benchley (1949), public domain,

Why is the terminology so confusing? .... p 57

For I am a Bear of Very Little Brain, and long words Bother me.

Milne AA, Winnie the Pooh (1926), Project Gutenberg, https://www.gutenberg.org/files/67098/67098-h/67098-h.htm, accessed 20 December 2022.

What if I can't stand another board member? .... p 63

I have been bent and broken, but – I hope – into a better shape.

Dickens C, Great Expectations (1860), Project Gutenberg, https://www.gutenberg.org/files/1400/1400-h/1400-h.htm, accessed 20 December 2022.

What do subcommittees do? .... p 67

'You know everything has to be examined and voted on by the committee,' said the cautious Secretary.

Holmes Sr OW, A Mortal Antipathy (1884), Project Gutenberg, https://www.gutenberg.org/files/2698/2698-h/2698-h.htm, accessed 20 December 2022.

Am I the only one feeling confused?.. p 71

'Really now you ask me,' said Alice, very much confused, 'I don't think-'

'Then you shouldn't talk,' said the Hatter.

Carroll L, Alice's Adventures in Wonderland (1865), Project Gutenberg, https://www.gutenberg.org/files/11/11-h/11-h.htm, accessed 20 December 2022.

Should I join if the organisation is a bit run down?............................ p 75

I like the dreams of the future better than the history of the past.

Jefferson T, Letter to John Adams (1816), Project Gutenberg, https://www.gutenberg.org/files/56035/56035-h/56035-h.htm, accessed 20 December 2022.

How much time will it take? .... p 79

Time travels in divers paces with divers persons.

Shakespeare W, As you like it (c1600), Project Gutenberg, https://www.gutenberg.org/files/1523/1523-h/1523-h.htm, accessed 20 December 2022.

Do I need to be a parent to be on a school board? .... p 83

It is like a barber's chair, that fits all buttocks...

Shakespeare W, All's well that ends well, (c1600), Project Gutenberg, https://www.gutenberg.org/files/1529/1529-h/1529-h.htm, accessed 20 December 2022.

How do I find out what's going on? .... p 87

I only ask for information.

Dickens C, David Copperfield (1849), Project Gutenberg, https://www.gutenberg.org/files/766/766-h/766-h.htm, accessed 20 December 2022.

Do I have to agree with everyone else? .... p 91

Quoting again from experience, a new birth, a change of heart, is perfectly possible...

Gandhi MK, Third Class in Indian Railways (1917), Project Gutenberg, https://www.gutenberg.org/files/24461/24461-h/24461-h.htm, accessed 20 December 2022.

What is a fiduciary duty? .... p 95

There is one thing, Emma, which a man can always do, if he chuses (sic), and that is, his duty; not by manoeuvring and finessing, but by vigour and resolution.

Austen J, Emma (1815),), Project Gutenberg, https://www.gutenberg.org/files/158/158-h/158-h.htm, accessed 20 December 2022.

What is 'formation'? .... p 99

...I will light in your heart the lamp of understanding, which shall not be put out....

Apocrypha, 2 Esdras 14.25, NRSV Bible

Is strategic planning really boring? .... p 103

One cannot have too large a party.

Austen J, Emma (1815), Project Gutenberg, https://www.gutenberg.org/files/158/158-h/158-h.htm, accessed 20 December 2022.

Will I get paid? .... p 107

How pleasant it is to have money, heigh ho!

How pleasant it is to have money.

Arthur Hugh Clough Dipsychus, in Poems of Arthur Hugh Clough (1898), Project Gutenberg, https://www.gutenberg.org/files/66689/66689-h/66689-h.htm, accessed 20 December 2022.

What if I feel overwhelmed? .... p 111

Take from my heart all painful anxiety.

McAuley C, (1778 – 1841) The Suscipe of Catherine McAuley, https://sistersofmercy.org/resource/the-suscipe-of-catherine-mcauley/, accessed 20 December 2022.

Who runs the place – the board or the Executive Director? .... p 115

I sell here, Sir, what all the world desires to have – POWER.

Boswell J & Hill GBN, Life of Johnson Vol 2, Project Gutenberg, https://www.gutenberg.org/ebooks/9072, accessed 20 December 2022.

The board Chair – how hard can it be to run a meeting? .... p 119

'Let there be few words and many deeds...'

Pallotti, St Vincent, 'We are salt and light blog' (Fr Frank Donio, SAC), https://www.wearesaltandlight.org/blog/2016/03/17/few-words-and-many-deeds, accessed 20 December 2022.

Will I have to 'lean in'? .... p 123

I must have my share in the conversation.

Austen J, Pride and Prejudice, Project Gutenberg,https://www.gutenberg.org/files/1342/1342-h/1342-h.htm, accessed 20 December 2022.

What on earth is an MPJP? .... p 127

'That sounds like nonsense, my dear.'

'May be so, my dear; but it may be very good law for all that.'

Scott W, Guy Mannering, Project Gutenberg, https://www.gutenberg.org/cache/epub/2590/pg2590.html, accessed 20 December 2022.

What happens if the members (or owners) disagree with the board's decision? .... p 131

We none of us expect to be in smooth water all our days.

Austen J, Persuasion, Project Gutenberg, https://www.gutenberg.org/files/105/105-h/105-h.htm, accessed 20 December 2022.

We've done 'mission', so can we start work now? .... p 135

Change your opinions, keep to your principles; change your leaves, keep intact your roots.

Victor Hugo V, Intellectual Autobiography (1907), Internet Archive, https://archive.org/stream/dli.bengal.10689.18214/10689.18214_djvu.txt, accessed 20 December 2022.

Did someone mention a pilgrimage? .... p 141

Redy to wenden on my pilgrimage

To Caunterbury with ful devout corage

Chaucer G, The Canterbury Tales (c1400), Project Gutenberg, https://www.gutenberg.org/files/22120/22120-h/22120-h.htm, accessed 20 December 2022.

Why does board history matter? ... p 145

The best prophet of the future is the past.

Byron GG, Journal (1821), Project Gutenberg, https://www.gutenberg.org/files/16609/16609-h/16609-h.htm, accessed 20 December 2022.

Did someone say synodality? .... p 149

Let us not soundproof our hearts; let us not remain barricaded in our certainties.

Pope Francis, 'Celebrating Synod means walking together on the same road', Vatican News, 2021, https://www.vaticannews.va/en/pope/news/2021-10/pope-celebrating-synod-means-walking-together-on-the-same-road.html, accessed 20 December 2022.

What's in it for me? .... p 153

When I'm not thanked at all, I'm thanked enough,

I've done my duty, and I've done no more.

Fielding H, Tom Thumb the Great (1731), Project Gutenberg, https://www.gutenberg.org/cache/epub/6828/pg6828.html, accessed 20 December 2022.

Suggested Links

Australian Institute of Company Directors (AICD)
aicd.companydirectors.com.au
Particularly the Not-for-Profit Governance Principles

Australian Securities and Investment Commission (ASIC)
asic.gov.au

Australian Charities and Not-for-profits Commission (ACNC)
acnc.gov.au

Australian Council for International Development
acfid.asn.au

Association of Ministerial PJPs
ampjp.org.au

Australian Catholic Bishops Conference
https://catholic.org.au/about-us/australian-catholic-bishops-conference

Conscious Governance
https://consciousgovernance.com/

CRA Catholic Religious Australia
https://www.catholicreligious.org.au/

Emerging Futures Collaborative
https://www.emergingfuturescollaborative.org.au/

Bibliography

Association of Ministerial PJPs, ampjp.org.au

ATNS, agreements, treaties and negotiated settlements project, Dja Dja Wurrung Recognition and Settlement Agreement https://database.atns.net.au/agreement.asp?EntityID=8300

Australian Catholic Safeguarding Limited (ACSL) https://www.acsltd.org.au/services/resource-hub/

Australian Government Federal Register of Legislation, Corporations Act, 2001 (Cth) https://www.legislation.gov.au/Details/C2019C00216

Australian Royal Commission into Institutional Responses to Child Sexual Abuse https://www.childabuseroyalcommission.gov.au/

Australian Institute of Company Directors, Director Tools https://www.aicd.com.au/tools-and-resources/director-tools.html

Board Committees, Australian Institute of Company Directors (AICD) https://www.aicd.com.au/board-of-directors/advisory/committee/role-of-the-board-committees.html

Companies Limited by Guarantee, Australian Charities and Not-for-profits Commission https://www.acnc.gov.au/for-charities/manage-your-charity/other-regulators/companies-limited-guarantee

Created and Loved, a guide for Catholic schools on identity and gender, Australian Catholic Bishops Conference https://bit.ly/CreatedandLoved

Djarra (Dja Dja Wurrung) Aboriginal Clans Corporation https://djadjawurrung.com.au/

Dja Dja Wurrung Recognition and Settlement Agreement, between Dja Dja Wurrung Clans Aboriginal Corporation and The State of Victoria, Bendigo, 28 March, 2013. https://files.justice.vic.gov.au/2021-06/vol1recognitionandsettlement agreement.pdf

Duties and Responsibilities of Boards and Board Directors, Your responsibilities as a director on a board, boards.vic.gov.au https://www.boards.vic.gov.au/duties-and-responsibilities-boards-and-board-directors

Insolvency for Directors, ASIC https://asic.gov.au/regulatory-resources/insolvency/insolvency-for-directors/

Laudauto Si', *On Care for our Common Home*, Second Encyclical Letter of Pope Francis, 24 May 2015. https://www.vatican.va/content/francesco/en/encyclicals/documents/papa-francesco_20150524_enciclica-laudato-si.html

***Laudato Si'* Action Platform** https://laudatosiactionplatform.org/

Loreto, Australia and South-East Asia, Mission https://www.loreto.org.au/mission-and-ministries/mission/

McMullen, Gabrielle and Oakley, Paul 'Ministerial PJPs advancing lay leadership in the Australian Church' *Australasian Catholic Record*, Vol. 97, (2020) No. 4, Oct 2020: 450-459 https://search.informit.com.au/documentSummary;dn=120741672379588;res=IELHSS

Pro bono Australia, What is a For-Purpose Brand Identity? https://probonoaustralia.com.au/news/2017/02/purpose-brand-identity/

Risk Assessment and Planning, Australian Government, Business https://business.gov.au/risk-management/risk-assessment-and-planning

Risk Management, Australian Institute of Company Directors https://www.aicd.com.au/risk-management/framework/plan/risk-management.html

Sandberg, S, *Lean in: Women, work and the will to lead*, Alfred P Knoph, 2013

Unincorporated Associations and ACNC Registration, Australian Charities and Not for profits Commission https://www.acnc.gov.au/for-charities/start-charity/you-start-charity/who-can-apply-be-registered/unincorporated

What is a not-for-profit? Australian Charities and Not-for-profits Commission https://www.acnc.gov.au/for-charities/start-charity/not-for-profit

Wright, M, 'The Development of the Ministerial Public Juridic Persons: Questions and Challenges', This presentation was given by Sr Mary Wright IBVM at the 52nd Annual Conference of the Canon Law Society of Australia and New Zealand. It was originally published in the CLSANZ Proceedings 2018 and is reproduced by the Association of Ministerial PJPs with the permission of the Editorial Board of the CLSANZ.

Your Company and the Law, Australian Securities and Investment Commission https://asic.gov.au/for-business/running-a-company/company-officeholder-duties/your-company-and-the-law/

Acknowledgements

This book exists because one day Michael McGirr deftly stopped me from whingeing at him about governance and mission matters, by telling me it was time to stop whingeing and go write a book instead. And so I did. Thank you, Michael, for providing me with the impetus to get fingers to keyboard, and for being so generous with your encouragement and time along the way.

Thanks also to publisher, Karen Tayleur, for her entirely unflappable help and advice, and to Juliette Hughes for ploughing on and providing her editing expertise despite my bafflement (which was no doubt very irritating) as to the appropriate use of commas.

Deep thanks to Karon Donnellon RSM, Virginia Bourke and Bishop Shane Mackinlay who all very generously read the full text and provided invaluable input.

Thanks too to Seamus, for playing with quotations with me; to Elizabeth and Patrick for believing in me, and to Tony for absolutely everything else.

Kathleen is a lawyer, mediator and facilitator. For the past 15 years, Kathleen has been a board director and board Chair of various faith-based, not-for-profit organisations, mainly involved in international and local aid programs and in education.

Kathleen has worked in private legal practice as well as in community-based law and has completed the Australian Institute of Company Directors (AICD) Course. She has also taught at the University of Melbourne Law School, where she lectured in mediation and dispute resolution.

www.ingramcontent.com/pod-product-compliance
Lightning Source LLC
Chambersburg PA
CBHW071606210326
41597CB00019B/3428
9781922484468